MW00721141

# THE LOW-CARB KITCHEN

★ ★

*Clean, Simple & Satisfying*

## 150

GREAT RECIPES

★

# CONTENTS

# INTRODUCTION

Low-carb, Paleo, Keto ... these are some of the words buzzing around in health-food circles at the moment. But why, and what's it all about? These styles of eating all share a basic desire to reduce carbohydrate in the diet. The reason for this is that when the body is deprived of blood sugar from carbs it looks to source energy elsewhere. Energy then comes from ketone bodies, which are produced when the body starts breaking down stored fat.

So, yes, cutting the carbs seems to be a good way to lose weight. Like any diet though, you have to stick with it in order to keep the weight off, and walking away from carbs altogether and forever is a tough ask for most of us. That's why in this book we place an emphasis on minimising, not eliminating carbs, on choosing 'good carbs', and on understanding how to enjoy low-carb food that's every bit as delicious as its carb-packed cousin.

Reducing 'bad carbs' that are quickly converted into sugar in the body means crossing white bread, pasta, white rice and fruit juices off the shopping list. But there are fantastic alternatives. 'Whole carbs' such as vegetables, whole fruit, legumes, potatoes, nuts, seeds and whole grains such as oats, quinoa and brown rice are a better choice. These foods are generally healthy, although some people on low-carb diets avoid potatoes, legumes and high-sugar fruits too. We have included them in small amounts in this book, readers who want a more strict application of the low-carb rule take note.

A hallmark of low-carb and Paleo diets is plenty of protein, which means an emphasis on meat, seafood and dairy, with all the wonderful nutrients that these foods contain. A good part of this book is given over to recipes where fish, chicken, lamb, beef or pork is the hero, helping you create delicious meals for the family out of these basic proteins. To avoid the usual white rice or potatoes on the side, in this book you'll find recipes for celeriac mash, broccoli mash, cauliflower rice and pumpkin mash – you are sure to be amazed at how easy these options are, and how delicious.

If you're worried about replacing 'fish and chips' on the dinnertime menu, don't be. We have you covered with recipes for baked fish, tangy salmon skewers, fishcakes, seafood stew and tandoori prawns. In the poultry section, there are pizza, curries, Moroccan-spiced stews, grilled chicken salads, and a Mediterranean-style roast that's sure to be a hit. If it's red meat you're after, you'll find plenty of inspiration from farmhouse stew and pork goulash to Thai beef salad, the perfect roast beef or sticky ribs.

Vegetables are the star in any healthy diet and in this section of the book we suggest myriad ways to prepare them hot or cold, spicy or roast. Beetroot lovers will enjoy the borscht or beetroot burgers; salad lovers will find many creative ideas for simple and more complex salads with low-carb dressings. We include dips, from tzatziki to baba ganoush, and sauces from kale pesto to chimichurri, to ensure your meals pack a flavoursome punch.

In the final section of this book, we celebrate desserts, because low-carb definitely does not mean no puddings allowed. Here you'll find new takes on old favourites such as ice cream, apple crumble or lemon posset, as well as some ideas that might be new to you such as frozen cheesecake or energy balls. We've got simple and everyday or fancy and impressive so take your pick from the wide range of ideas on offer in this book.

Let's save the last word for breakfast – the first section in this book, and arguably the most important meal of the day. Check out the recipes here for inspiration on how to make the switch from sugar-loaded cereal to cylinder-firing proteins and good carbs to help you sail through the day.

# BREAKFAST

# HOMEMADE GRANOLA

## INGREDIENTS

¼ cup (40g, 1½ oz) ground flaxseed

¾ cup (185ml, 6fl oz) water

3½ cups (315g, 11oz) rolled oats (not instant)

⅔ cup (80g, 3oz) pecans, roughly chopped

⅔ cup (80g, 3oz) walnuts, roughly chopped

⅔ cup (80g, 3oz) almonds, roughly chopped

½ cup (65g, 2oz) pumpkin seeds (pepitas)

¼ cup (30g, 1oz) sunflower seeds

½ cup (180g, 6oz) honey

½ cup (180g, 6oz) agave syrup

2 tbsps melted and cooled coconut oil

½ tsp cinnamon

½ tsp salt

½ cup (95g, 3oz) low-sugar dried apricots, chopped

## METHOD

1. Preheat oven to 150°C (300°F, Gas Mark 2) and line a large flat baking tray with baking paper.

2. Mix together the flaxseed and the water and set aside.

3. Combine all the other ingredients together, except the dried apricots, and stir to mix thoroughly, then stir through the flaxseed mixture.

4. Spread the nut mix evenly over the baking paper and bake in the oven for 50 minutes, or until lightly browned.

5. Allow to cool completely, then break apart and stir through the dried apricots.

6. Store in an airtight container up to 2 weeks.

# GREEN SMOOTHIE

## INGREDIENTS

1 cup (30g, 1oz)
spinach, chopped

½ cup (15g, ½ oz)
silverbeet, chopped

½ cup (15g, ½ oz)
kale, chopped

1 banana (frozen),
chopped

1 apple, chopped

1 pear, chopped

1½ cups (375ml,
13fl oz) coconut water

## METHOD

1. Place all the ingredients into a blender.

2. Blend together until thoroughly combined and smooth.

3. Serve.

# ACAI BERRY SMOOTHIE

## INGREDIENTS

1 cup (100g, 3½ oz) frozen blueberries (reserve ¼ cup for garnish)

1 banana (frozen), chopped

⅓ cup (80ml, 3fl oz) coconut water

¼ cup (20g, ¾ oz) rolled oats (reserve 2 tsps for garnish)

2 tbsps dark chocolate, shaved

2 tsps acai powder

## METHOD

1. Place blueberries, banana, coconut water, oats, 1 tablespoon of chocolate and the acai powder into a blender.

2. Puree until thoroughly combined and smooth.

3. Serve garnish with reserved blueberries, oats and chocolate.

# WHOLEGRAIN TOAST WITH HOMEMADE CREAM CHEESE

## INGREDIENTS

4 slices wholegrain
bread

1 pear, cored and
thinly sliced

2 tsps flaxseeds

2 tbsps hazelnuts,
chopped

2 sprigs fresh oregano

4 tsps olive oil

**Cream cheese**
(makes approx. 1 cup)

1 cup (260g, 9oz)
silken tofu

2 tbsps white chia
seeds, finely ground

¼ cup (30g, 1oz) raw
cashews, roughly
chopped

2 tsps agave syrup

2 tbsps water

Salt and pepper,
to taste

## METHOD

1.  Place all the ingredients for the cream cheese in a blender.

2.  Blend until thoroughly combined and smooth and creamy.

3.  Place in the refrigerator for 2 hours to thicken to a cream cheese consistency.

4.  When ready to eat remove from the refrigerator and season to taste with salt and pepper.

5.  To assemble, toast the slices of bread.

6.  Spread 2 tablespoons of the cream cheese over each slice of toast.

7.  Top with slices of pear, a sprinkling of flaxseeds and chopped hazelnuts and some oregano leaves.

8.  Drizzle a teaspoon of olive oil over each.

9.  Serve.

# QUINOA APPLE PORRIDGE

## INGREDIENTS

1 cup (170g, 6oz) quinoa (any colour)

1 tsp coconut oil

2 cups (500ml, 1pt) boiling water

1 red apple, peeled and cubed

½ cup (125ml, 4fl oz) low-fat soy or almond milk

½ cup (60g, 2oz) pecans, roughly chopped

1 tbsp maple syrup

1 tsp cinnamon

## METHOD

1   Rinse the quinoa and soak in a bowl of water for at least 1 hour, then drain before use.

2   Heat the oil in a medium saucepan over medium-high heat and add the quinoa. Stir for 1 minute, then add the boiling water.

3   Bring to a boil then reduce the heat to low.

4   Stir through the apple then let it cook, covered, for 15 minutes, until the water is absorbed.

5   Stir through the milk, pecans, maple syrup and cinnamon.

6.   Serve.

# YOGHURT GRANOLA POTS

## INGREDIENTS

1 cup (250ml, 8fl oz) low-fat yoghurt

¾ cup (90g, 3oz) granola (see recipe page 8)

1 large banana, sliced

½ cup (50g, 2oz) fresh blueberries

## METHOD

1. Place ¼ cup yoghurt each into the bottom of the two serving glasses.

2. Place a dessertspoon of granola on top of each.

3. Layer over another ¼ cup yoghurt over the granola.

4. Top each with the rest of the granola, half the sliced banana and half the blueberries.

5. Serve.

# VEGGIE MINI QUICHE

## INGREDIENTS

**Pastry**

1 cup (100g, 3½ oz) coconut flour

½ tsp salt

3 eggs

¾ cup (185ml, 6fl oz) butter or ghee, melted.

**Filling**

8 eggs

1 cup (225g, 8oz) low-fat cottage cheese

½ cup (120g, 4oz) reduced fat feta

½ red capsicum, chopped

¼ tsp salt

¼ tsp pepper

6 florets of broccoli, halved

Parsley, to garnish

## METHOD

1. Place flour and salt in a large bowl and stir through the eggs and butter until a dough forms. Add more flour if dough is too sticky.

2. Knead dough for a minute then form into a flattened disc. Wrap in plastic and place in refrigerator for 30 minutes to chill.

3. Remove the dough from the refrigerator.

4. Preheat oven to 200°C (400°F, Gas Mark 6) and lightly grease 12 mini quiche tins.

5. Roll out the dough until about 1cm (½ in) thick. Cut rounds out to fill your quiche tins. Prick bottom of crust with a fork and bake for 10 minutes.

6. Remove from oven and reduce the heat to 190°C (375°F, Gas Mark 5).

7. Lightly beat the eggs, then stir through the cottage cheese, feta, capsicum and salt and pepper.

8. To assemble, half fill each case with the egg mixture and then gently place a half-floret into the middle of each case, flat side up.

9. Bake in the oven for 30 minutes or until the tops begin to brown.

10. Remove and let cool.

11. Serve garnished with chopped parsley.

# LOW-CARB CINNAMON PORRIDGE

## INGREDIENTS

4 tbsps white chia seeds, ground

4 tbsps ground flaxseed

3 cups (750ml, 24fl oz) low-fat soy or almond milk

1 red apple, cored and sliced

¼ cup (30g, 1oz) walnuts, roughly chopped

½ tsp cinnamon

1½ tbsps maple or agave syrup

## METHOD

1. Two hours before serving, mix together the ground chia seeds, flaxseed and milk. Set aside to thicken.

2. Pour the thickened porridge into a small saucepan and heat gently over medium heat for 10 minutes or until just bubbling.

3. Remove from heat and ladle into two serving bowls. Place the apple and chopped walnuts on top.

4. Sprinkle half the cinnamon over each and drizzle the syrup over each to taste.

# COCONUT CHIA BREAKFAST BOWL

## INGREDIENTS

¼ cup (70ml, 2½ fl oz) coconut milk

½ cup (125ml, 4fl oz) coconut water

1 tbsp maple syrup or agave syrup

¼ cup (40g, 1½ oz) chia seeds (any colour)

⅔ cup (125g, 4oz) strawberries, quartered

¼ cup (25g, 1oz) fresh blueberries

3 tbsps flaked almonds

3 tbsps pomegranate seeds

1 tbsp shredded coconut

2 sprigs mint leaves, to garnish

## METHOD

1. The evening before, mix the coconut milk, coconut water, maple syrup and chia seeds together in a bowl. Cover and place in the refrigerator overnight to let the chia seeds soften and absorb the liquid.

2. In the morning, divide the soaked chia seeds between two bowls.

3. Top with the rest of the ingredients and garnish with the mint leaves.

4. Serve.

# VEGGIE FRITTERS WITH YOGHURT SAUCE

## INGREDIENTS

**Yoghurt sauce**

1 cup (250ml, 8fl oz) low-fat Greek yoghurt

1 garlic clove, minced

Pinch salt and pepper

**Fritters**

1 small head cauliflower, chopped into small pieces

2 cups (60g, 2oz) fresh spinach, chopped

2 spring onions, finely chopped

3 eggs, lightly beaten

½ cup (60g, 2oz) chickpea flour

2 tbsps flatleaf parsley, finely chopped

1 clove garlic, crushed

1 tsp salt

Freshly ground pepper

2 tbsps olive oil, for frying

¼ cup (50g, 2oz) Greek yoghurt

## METHOD

1. Mix together the yoghurt, garlic, salt and pepper in small bowl. Place the sauce in the refrigerator to chill while making the fritters.

2. Boil the cauliflower in large pot for 4 minutes, until softened. Drain and mash it well but do not puree it.

3. In a large bowl, combine the spinach, spring onions, eggs, flour, parsley, garlic and salt. Give it a good couple of grinds of pepper as well. Add in the cauliflower and mix well. Shape small handfuls of the mixture into balls and flatten slightly.

4. Heat a dash of olive oil in a large frying pan on medium heat and fry the fritters a couple at a time. Don't overcrowd the pan. Cook on each side for 5 minutes or until browned all over.

5. Serve with a side of fresh Greek yoghurt.

# GRANOLA BARS

## INGREDIENTS

1½ cups (130g, 4½ oz) oats

1 tsp baking powder

½ tsp bicarbonate of soda

½ tsp salt

½ tsp cinnamon

½ cup (80g, 3oz) light brown sugar

1 cup (125g, 4oz) almond flakes

1 cup (125g, 4oz) pecans, chopped

½ cup (60g, 2oz) sunflower seeds

¾ cup (95g, 3oz) pumpkin seeds (pepitas)

1 cup (190g, 7oz) dried apricots, chopped

1 egg

2 tbsps coconut oil

¼ cup (40g, 1½ oz) unsweetened apple sauce (use baby food – no preservatives or sweeteners!)

¼ cup (80g, 3oz) maple syrup

## METHOD

1. Preheat oven to 175°C (350°F, Gas Mark 4) and line a slice tray with greased baking paper.

2. Roughly chop the oats in a blender then add to a large bowl and mix together with all the other dry ingredients.

3. Mix together all the other ingredients and then mix through into the dry ingredients until thoroughly combined.

4. Press mixture into the slice tin.

5. Bake for 25 minutes, or until browned.

6. Cut into desired shapes once cooled.

# OVERNIGHT OATS

### INGREDIENTS

¾ cup (200ml, 7fl oz) low-fat Greek yoghurt

2 tbsps white chia seeds

¼ cup (20g, ¾ oz) oats

½ cup (125ml, 4fl oz) almond or soy milk

2 tbsps maple syrup

½ tsp vanilla extract

1 cup (200g, 7oz) strawberries

½ cup (60g, 2oz) fresh raspberries

½ cup (50g, 2oz) fresh blueberries

¼ cup (60g, 2oz) almonds, roughly chopped

2 sprigs mint, to garnish

### METHOD

1. Mix together the yoghurt, chia seeds, oats, milk, maple syrup and vanilla in a medium bowl.

2. Divide between two serving glasses and place in the refrigerator overnight.

3. Serve with the berries on top and mint to garnish.

# BREAKFAST BURRITO

## INGREDIENTS

2 tsps olive oil

1 small waxy potato, cut into small cubes

2 cups (60g, 2oz) baby spinach

1 spring onion, finely chopped

1 tsp cumin

1 tsp ground coriander

1 x 400g (14oz) can butter beans, drained and rinsed

1 large avocado, cubed

150g (5oz) low-fat feta

¼ cup (25g, 1oz) Parmesan cheese, grated

3 eggs

¼ cup (60ml, 2fl oz) low-fat milk

3 tbsps water

Salt and pepper to taste

## METHOD

1. Heat the olive oil in a small non-stick frying pan over medium heat. Fry the potato cubes for 5 minutes until browned.

2. Add the spinach, spring onion, cumin, coriander and butter beans and fry for a further 2 minutes. (you might need to add the spinach in two batches)

3. Drain any excess liquid from the spinach and place the mix in a bowl and gently stir the avocado, feta and half the Parmesan through. Set aside.

4. Wipe the pan clean to reuse for the burrito wraps.

5. To make the burrito wraps, beat the eggs in a large bowl and mix well with milk, water and a pinch of salt and pepper.

6. Heat the frying pan on low.

7. Pour out half the mixture into the pan to form a thin, plain omelette.

8. Allow it to cook well and when it begins to come away from the pan on its own, flip over and cook the other side.

9. Once cooked, lay the omelette on a plate and repeat with the rest of the egg mixture.

10. Divide the bean mix between the two omelettes, then roll them up burrito style. Serve sprinkled with the rest of the Parmesan cheese.

# HOMEMADE MUESLI

## INGREDIENTS

1 cup (125g, 4oz) almonds, flaked

1 cup (90g, 3oz) coconut flakes

1 cup (125g, 4oz) pecans, chopped

1 cup (125g, 4oz) walnuts, chopped

1 cup (90g, 3oz) rolled oats

½ cup (60g, 2oz) sunflower seeds

1 tbsp brown sugar

1 tsp cinnamon

½ tsp nutmeg

1 cup (160g, 6oz) dried cranberries

## METHOD

1.  Preheat oven to 180°C (350°F, Gas Mark 4) and line a large baking tray with baking paper.

2.  Mix all ingredients, except the cranberries , together in a large bowl.

3.  Spread evenly over the baking paper.

4.  Bake in the oven for 8 minutes then remove and let cool.

5.  Stir through the cranberries.

6.  Serve with soy or almond milk and slices of fresh fruit.

**Note:** Will keep in an airtight container for 2 weeks.

SERVES 2 ★ PREP 10MIN ★ COOK TIME 5MIN

# FRENCH TOAST

## INGREDIENTS

4 eggs

⅓ cup (80ml, 3fl oz) low-fat milk (soy or dairy)

1 tsp ground cinnamon

Olive oil spray

4 slices wholegrain sourdough

1 small blood orange, sliced

⅓ cup (30g, 1oz) fresh blueberries

4 strawberries, halved

2 tbsps agave syrup

## METHOD

1. Lightly beat the eggs with the milk and cinnamon.

2. Spray a non-stick frying pan with olive oil and heat over medium heat.

3. Soak each piece of sourdough thoroughly in the egg mixture.

4. Fry the egg-soaked bread slices for 1 minute on each side or until browned.

5. Serve warm with slices of orange, blueberries, strawberries and with agave syrup drizzled over.

# SHAKSHOUKA

## INGREDIENTS

1 tbsp olive oil

1 small red onion, chopped

1 small red capsicum, chopped

2 tbsps pickled jalapeño chilli, finely chopped

2 garlic cloves, crushed

1 tsp cumin

1 tsp ground oregano

1 tsp sweet paprika

1 x 400g (14oz) can chopped tomatoes

1 x 400g (14oz) can kidney beans

4 eggs

2 tbsps coriander, chopped, to garnish

## METHOD

1. Preheat oven to 180°C (350°F, Gas Mark 4).

2. Heat the olive oil in a medium heavy oven-proof frying pan over medium heat.

3. Fry the onion, capsicum, chilli and garlic for 5 minutes, or until the onion is softened.

4. Stir through the cumin, oregano and paprika for 1 minute.

5. Add the tomatoes and kidney beans and bring to a boil.

6. Reduce heat to a low simmer and cook for 15 minutes.

7. Remove from the heat.

8. Make four hollows in the mixture and gently crack the eggs into them, being careful not to break the yolks.

9. Transfer the frying pan to the oven and bake for 10 minutes, or until the eggs are cooked to your liking.

10. Let sit for 5 minutes once out of the oven.

11. Serve garnished with coriander.

# BREAKFAST BAGEL

## INGREDIENTS

1 tbsp rice flour

1 tbsp tapioca flour

1 large onion, thickly sliced into rings

2 tbsps olive oil

2 wholegrain bagels, halved

4 butter lettuce leaves

300g (10oz) sliced prosciutto

½ cup (15g, ½ oz) watercress

Salt and pepper, to taste

## METHOD

1. Stir together the flours, lightly season them and then toss with the onion rings so they are lightly coated.

2. Heat a small non-stick frying pan over medium heat. Heat the olive oil and then fry the onion slices for 8 minutes until they are softened but slightly crunchy on the outside.

3. Remove from the pan and drain on absorbent paper.

4. Lightly toast the bagel halves.

5. Layer each bagel with 2 lettuce leaves, half the prosciutto, half the onion and half the cress.

6. Serve.

# SALMON AVOCADO ON RYE

## INGREDIENTS

1 large avocado

½ tsp lemon juice

½ tsp dill, chopped

Salt and pepper, to taste

4 slices rye bread

400g (14oz) smoked salmon slices

1 small red onion, thinly sliced

## METHOD

1. Mash together the avocado with the lemon juice and dill. Season with salt and pepper.

2. Divide the avocado mash between the four slices and spread each slice with it.

3. Top with the smoked salmon slices.

4. Garnish with red onion slices to taste.

# STUFFED BUCKWHEAT PANCAKES

## INGREDIENTS

### Pancakes

100g (3½ oz) unsalted butter

¾ cup (90g, 3oz) buckwheat flour

¼ cup (30g, 1oz) plain flour

3 eggs

½ tsp salt

1⅔ cups (400ml, 13fl oz) low-fat soy or almond milk

### Filling

½ cup (60g, 2oz) grated Parmesan

2 cups (500g, 1lb 2oz) cherry tomatoes, halved

400g (14oz) prosciutto

2 cups (60g, 2oz) loosely packed baby spinach

2 cups (60g, 2oz) loosely packet rocket

¼ cup (10g, ¼ oz) roughly chopped parsley

## METHOD

1. Preheat the oven to 60°C (140°F) for keeping the cooked pancakes warm.

2. Melt half the butter and combine in a medium bowl with the flours, eggs, salt and half the milk. Whisk together and add the rest of the milk a small amount at a time until the mixture is smooth.

3. Let mixture sit for at least 30 minutes.

4. Melt 1 tablespoon of the remaining butter in a large non-stick frying pan and pour a quarter of the mixture into the pan.

5. Cook the pancake on one side for 2 minutes or until the edges start to brown and come away from the pan.

6. Carefully flip over and sprinkle a quarter of the Parmesan over the pancake. Let it cook for another 30 seconds or so and carefully transfer to a serving plate and put one quarter of the remaining filling ingredients over one half of the pancake, then fold the other half of the pancake over the filling.

7. Place in the oven to warm while you repeat the steps with the remaining batter and ingredients.

SERVES 2 ★ PREP 10min ★ COOK TIME 4min

# POACHED EGGS WITH THE LOT

## INGREDIENTS

4 slices wholegrain sourdough

1 large avocado, sliced

¾ cup (170g, 6oz) cream cheese (see recipe page 12)

4 eggs (fresh is best for poaching)

White vinegar

2 tbsps pumpkin seeds (pepitas)

1 tbsp parsley, roughly chopped

## METHOD

1. To poach the eggs, add a small dash of vinegar to a pan of steadily simmering water – about 5cm (2in) deep.

2. Crack each egg gently into a small shallow dish and use this to slide them into the water one at a time.

3. Cook for 2½ to 3 minutes for a runny yolk.

4. Cook for 3½ to 4 minutes for a set yolk.

5. Gently lift the eggs out with a slotted spoon and drain on a paper towel.

6. Spread the sourdough slices with the cream cheese and place the avocado slices on top.

7. Place the eggs on top of the avocado and then garnish with a sprinkling of pepitas and chopped parsley.

# MUSHROOM SCRAMBLE

## INGREDIENTS

3 large eggs

1 tsp olive oil

1 spring onion, sliced

1 small garlic clove, crushed

1 cup (100g, 3½ oz) oyster mushrooms, sliced

1 cup (100g, 3½ oz) button mushrooms, sliced

1 tbsp flat-leaf parsley, roughly chopped

Salt and pepper, to taste

## METHOD

1. Whisk the eggs thoroughly for at least one minute to make them light and fluffy.

2. Heat the oil in a medium non-stick frying pan over medium heat.

3. Add the spring onion, garlic and mushrooms and fry for two minutes or until the mushrooms are slightly browned. Remove from the pan and set aside.

4. Reduce the heat to medium-low and pour in the eggs.

5. Cook them for 2 minutes or until done to your liking by slowly dragging your wooden spoon from the edges of the pan into the middle. Don't 'scramble' them too much or they lose their fluffiness.

6. Add the mushroom mixture and gently mix it through.

7. Serve garnished with parsley and add salt and pepper to taste.

SERVES 3 ★ PREP 15MIN ★ COOK TIME 30MIN

# EGGS FLORENTINE

**INGREDIENTS**

2 tbsps butter or ghee

1 large brown onion, chopped

750g (1½ lb) fresh spinach, chopped

¾ cup (90g, 3oz) grated Swiss cheese

3 tbsps Dijon mustard

⅓ cup (80ml, 3fl oz) low-fat cream

Pinch paprika

Pinch nutmeg

6 eggs

Salt and pepper, to taste

**METHOD**

1. Preheat oven to 190°C (375°F, Gas Mark 5).
2. In a medium frying pan, melt the butter over medium heat.
3. Fry the onion for 5 minutes until softened.
4. Stir in the spinach, 1 cup at a time, until softened. Remove from the heat and set aside.
5. In a medium bowl, whisk together the cheese, mustard, cream, paprika and nutmeg.
6. Layer the spinach mixture in the bottom of a baking dish. Make 6 small wells in the mixture and gently break the eggs into each one.
7. Pour the cheese mixture over the top.
8. Bake in the oven for 25 minutes.
9. Let sit for 5 minutes before serving.

# BIRCHER MUESLI

## INGREDIENTS

½ cup (40g, 1½ oz) rolled oats

1 tsp chia seeds

1 cup (250ml, 8fl oz) almond milk (or your preferred milk)

1 tsp maple syrup

2 tbsps shredded coconut

2 tbsps pistachio nuts, chopped

1 fig, cut into pieces

Frozen berries, to serve

## METHOD

1. Combine oats, chia seeds and milk in a jar or other sealable container.

2. Shake well and place in the refrigerator overnight.

3. Serve with shredded coconut, fresh and frozen fruit and nuts.

# STUFFED MUSHROOMS

## INGREDIENTS

2 tsps olive oil

1 small onion, finely chopped

4 large portobello mushrooms, wiped and stems removed and finely chopped

120g (4oz) low-fat feta cheese

120g (4oz) low-fat cream cheese

¼ cup (10g, ¼ oz) parsley, finely chopped

Salt and pepper, to taste

## METHOD

1. Preheat oven to 180°C (350°F, Gas Mark 4) and line a baking tray with baking paper.

2. In a small frying pan, heat the olive oil over medium heat.

3. Fry the onion and chopped mushroom stems for 5 minutes until onion is softened.

4. Remove from heat and set aside.

5. In a medium bowl, combine the cheeses, half the parsley and the onion mixture.

6. Spoon the cheese mixture into the four mushrooms and place on the baking tray.

7. Bake for 20 minutes or until browned on top.

8. Serve warm garnished with the rest of the parsley.

# BREAKFAST BOWL

## INGREDIENTS

2 cups (60g, 2oz) tightly packed mixed salad leaves

200g (7oz) smoked salmon

1 small avocado

4 eggs

White vinegar

1 radish, thinly sliced

1 tbsp black sesame seeds

1 tbsp white sesame seeds

2 lemon wedges

## METHOD

1. Split the salad leaves between two serving bowls.

2. Place half the smoked salmon on top in each bowl.

3. Slice the avocado and place half in each bowl.

4. To poach the eggs, add a small dash of vinegar to a pan of steadily simmering water – about 5cm (2in) deep.

5. Crack each egg gently into a small shallow dish and use this to slide them into the water one at a time.

6. Cook for 2½ to 3 minutes for a runny yolk.
   Cook for 3½ to 4 minutes for a set yolk.

7. Gently lift the eggs out with a slotted spoon and drain on a paper towel.

8. Place 2 eggs in each bowl to the side of the avocado.

9. Place the sliced radish on top.

10. Garnish with the sesame seeds and lemon wedges.

# FISH AND SEAFOOD

# BAKED SALMON FILLET

## INGREDIENTS

1 medium carrot, sliced

1 medium parsnip, sliced

4 sprigs thyme

2 tsps lemon juice

2 tsps olive oil

Salt and pepper, to taste

1 x 400g (14oz) salmon fillet, skin removed, deboned

¼ cup (50ml, 2fl oz) vegetable stock

## METHOD

1. Preheat the oven to 200°C (400°F, Gas Mark 6).

2. Cut out a piece of baking paper large enough to completely enclose the salmon fillet and long enough to be tied up at the ends.

3. Parboil the vegetables for 3 minutes then place in the bottom of the baking paper. Place the salmon on top.

4. Mix together the thyme, lemon juice, olive oil and a good couple of grinds of salt and pepper and spread over the salmon fillet.

5. Pour the stock over the salmon.

6. Enclose the salmon and tie at the ends. Place the parcel on a baking tray.

7. Bake in the oven for 20 minutes or until the fish is just cooked through.

8. Serve warm with the baked vegetables.

# SESAME SEARED SCALLOPS

### INGREDIENTS

1 tbsp lemon juice

1 tbsp fresh ginger, minced

1 garlic clove, crushed

1 small spring onion, finely chopped

½ tbsp rice wine vinegar

½ tbsp sesame oil

1 tbsp canola oil

2 tbsps soy sauce

½ tbsp sake (or dry sherry)

400g (14oz) sea scallops, trimmed

2 tbsp white sesame seeds

2 tsp black sesame seeds

½ tsp chilli flakes (to taste)

### METHOD

1.  In a small bowl, thoroughly mix together the ginger, garlic, onion, vinegar, sesame oil, half the canola, soy, and the sake. Set aside.

2.  Pat the scallops dry with a paper towel.

3.  Mix the sesame seeds and chilli flakes together in a small plate or bowl and coat the top and bottom of each scallop in them.

4.  Heat the rest of the canola oil in a frying pan to medium-high heat. Then add half the ginger-soy liquid and immediately place the scallops in the pan.

5.  Fry each side for around 1 minute or until they start to brown.

6.  Serve immediately.

# SPICY FISHCAKES

## INGREDIENTS

200g (7oz) whiting fillets (or hake), deboned

2 tbsps Thai red curry paste

1 tbsp fish sauce

½ tsp brown sugar

1 tsp lime zest

2 kaffir lime leaves, spine removed and finely shredded

1 tbsp oyster sauce

1 tsp rice wine vinegar

Salt, to taste

4 tbsps cornflour

¼ cup (60ml, 2fl oz) canola oil

Lime slices and chopped tomatoes, to serve

1 tbsp dill, chopped, to garnish

## METHOD

1. Place the fish, curry paste, fish sauce and sugar in a blender and process until smooth.

2. Transfer the mixture to a bowl and stir in the lime zest, lime leaves, oyster sauce, vinegar and a pinch of salt. Mix thoroughly to ensure all ingredients are thoroughly combined.

3. Add half the cornflour and mix in thoroughly to help it stick together a bit more. Add the rest of the flour if needed.

4. Form dessertspoon-sized portions into rough balls.

5. Heat the oil in a shallow frying pan over high heat. Once the oil is hot, reduce to medium and fry the cakes for 5 minutes on each side, or until they are browned and cooked through.

6. Serve warm with lime slices and tomatoes, garnished with dill.

# POACHED SNAPPER WITH CELERIAC MASH

## INGREDIENTS

1 medium celeriac

200g (7oz) yellow beans, trimmed

50g (2oz) butter

Salt, to taste

300g (10oz) snapper fillets

1 tbsp flat-leaf parsley, chopped

½ tbsp capers, finely chopped

½ tsp lemon juice

1 tbsp olive oil

Pepper, to taste

Handful nasturtium leaves, rinsed (optional)

Sprig wild garlic flowers for garnish (optional)

## METHOD

1. Peel the celeriac and cut into 2cm (1in) chunks.

2. Boil celeriac in a large pot of salted water for 15-20 minutes or until tender. Remove from pot and then boil the beans in the same water for 2 minutes.

3. Mash the celeriac with the butter until smooth. Add salt to taste.

4. Remove the beans from the pot and reserve the water.

5. Pour the reserved water into a deep frying pan large enough to hold the fillets. Bring the liquid to simmering, then add the fish. Add more boiling water as needed to just cover the fish. Simmer over low heat for 8 minutes.

6. Divide the mash and beans over two plates and place the fish on top.

7. Mix together the parsley, capers, lemon juice, oil and a good grind of salt and pepper and drizzle over the fillets.

8. Garnish with nasturtium leaves and garlic flowers, if using.

# MEDITERRANEAN TUNA SALAD

## INGREDIENTS

2 tbsps olive oil

1 tbsp balsamic vinegar

½ tbsp lemon juice

Salt and pepper, to taste

1 large red capsicum, chopped

½ cup (25g, 1oz) semi-sun-dried tomatoes, chopped

3 large spring onions, sliced on an angle

1½ cups (210g, 8oz) Kalamata olives, pitted and halved

150g (5oz) baby spinach leaves

200g (7oz) green beans, trimmed and cut into 4cm (1½ in) pieces

1 cup (45g, 1½ oz) flat-leaf parsley, roughly chopped

1 x 400g (14oz) can tuna in spring water, drained and flaked

250g (9oz) feta cheese, crumbled

½ lemon, zested in thin strips, to garnish

## METHOD

1.  Whisk together the olive oil, vinegar, lemon juice and a good couple of grinds of salt and pepper.

2.  Place the rest of the ingredients in a large salad bowl.

3.  Pour over the dressing and mix everything together thoroughly

4.  Garnish with lemon peel strips.

SERVES 2 ★ PREP 15MIN ★ COOK TIME 25MIN

# BAKED SALMON ON CAULIFLOWER RICE

## INGREDIENTS

¼ cup (60ml, 2fl oz) soy sauce

1 tbsp rice wine vinegar

2 tbsps fresh ginger, grated

2 tbsps lime juice

½ tbsp chilli sauce

2 garlic cloves, crushed

2 x 150g (5oz) salmon steaks, skin on.

1 small head cauliflower

1 tbsp sesame oil

200g (7oz) button mushrooms, chopped

2 spring onions, sliced

## METHOD

1.  Preheat oven to 220°C (425°F, Gas Mark 7).

2.  In a small bowl, mix together the soy sauce, vinegar, ginger, lime, chilli and garlic. Place the salmon steaks in a baking dish and pour the sauce over the top. Bake for 15 minutes or until the salmon is cooked through. Cover and set aside.

3.  Break the cauliflower into pieces then place them in a food processor. Pulse until the cauliflower begins to resemble rice.

4.  Heat the oil in a large frying pan over medium heat. Add the mushrooms and cook for 5 minutes. Add the cauliflower, cover and cook for 5 minutes.

5.  Pour 1½ tablespoons of the sauce from the baking dish over the top of the rice and gently stir through. Heat for a further minute.

6.  Serve the salmon steaks on top of the cauliflower, garnished with spring onion.

# FISH AND SEAFOOD STEW

## INGREDIENTS

1 tbsp olive oil

2 shallots, sliced

300g (10oz) waxy potatoes, peeled and cut into 2cm (1in) cubes

2 garlic cloves, crushed

4 cups (1L, 2pt) fish or vegetable stock

½ cup (125ml, 4fl oz) dry white wine

1 large lemon, zested and juiced

300g (10oz) bass or hake fillets, cut into chunks

300g (10oz) squid, cut into 2cm (1in) strips

500g (1lb 2oz) mussels, cleaned and debearded

¼ cup (10g, ¼ oz) coriander

## METHOD

1. Heat the olive oil in a large heavy pot over medium heat. Add the shallots, potatoes and garlic and fry for 5 minutes, until the shallots have softened.

2. Add the stock, wine, lemon juice, fish and squid and bring to a boil.

3. Reduce the heat and simmer gently for 5 minutes.

4. Add the mussels, put a lid on the pot and cook for another 5 minutes, until the mussels are cooked.

5. Remove the mussels and stir through half the coriander and lemon zest. Let it simmer for a further 5 minutes.

6. Gently remove the mussels from their shells and stir into the stew.

7. Serve garnished with the rest of the coriander and lemon zest and crusty bread on the side.

# TUNA NIÇOISE

## INGREDIENTS

2 bunches asparagus, ends trimmed

1 x 400g (14oz) can tuna in spring water, drained

1 red onion, thinly sliced

5 small eggs, hard-boiled, peeled and halved

2 cups (60g, 2oz) baby spinach, roughly chopped

5 Roma tomatoes, cut into wedges

⅓ cup (15g, ½ oz) fresh basil, shredded

### Dressing

1 tbsp Dijon mustard

½ tbsp red wine vinegar

1 tbsp olive oil

1 small garlic clove, crushed

Salt and pepper

½ tbsp lemon juice

## METHOD

1.  Place all the dressing ingredients in a small jar and shake to combine. Set aside

2.  Steam the asparagus for 4 minutes until tender but still firm and let cool for 10 minutes.

3.  To make the salad, combine all the salad ingredients evenly in individual serving bowls.

4.  Pour over dressing to taste.

# GRILLED OCTOPUS SALAD

## INGREDIENTS

1 cup (250ml, 8fl oz) dry white wine

2 cups (500ml, 1pt) water

1 small onion, chopped

½ celery stalk, chopped

1 small carrot, chopped

2 garlic cloves, crushed

1 bay leaf

½ tbsp fennel seeds

500g (1lb 2oz) whole octopus, trimmed (ask your fishmonger to do this)

2 tsps olive oil

Salt and pepper, to taste

Lemon wedges to serve

**Salad**

1 medium Lebanese cucumber, halved and sliced

1 punnet red cherry tomatoes, halved

1 cup (30g, 1oz) baby spinach

1 small red capsicum, seeded and sliced

1 cup (140g, 5oz) black olives

1 red onion, thinly sliced

## METHOD

1.  Add the wine, water, onion, celery, carrot, garlic, bay leaf and fennel seeds to a medium pot and bring to the boil. Lower the octopus in, tentacles first. Reduce heat and simmer for 1 hour.

2.  Remove octopus and boil off the remaining liquid until almost syrupy. Strain and set the liquid aside. Cut and separate the tentacles.

3.  Arrange the salad ingredients on serving plates.

4.  Heat a grill pan to high.

5.  Season the octopus with syrup, oil and salt and pepper. Grill for 3 minutes, turning all the while.

6.  Serve over the salad. Drizzle with extra oil and serve with lemon wedges on the side.

    **Note:** To save time, use store-bought vegetable stock and skip the first step of this recipe, or simply buy pre-cooked octopus from the deli and assemble the salad using the remaining ingredients.

# MUSSELS WITH WHITE WINE AND HERBS

## INGREDIENTS

2 tbsps olive oil

½ small celery rib, chopped

¼ cup (60ml, 2fl oz) dry white wine

1 cup (250ml, 8fl oz) fish or vegetable stock

750g (1½ lb) fresh mussels, washed and debearded

3 tbsps flat-leaf parsley, roughly chopped

2 tsps fresh thyme, chopped

Salt and pepper, to taste

Lemon wedges, to garnish

## METHOD

1. In a large pot, heat the oil over medium heat. Cook the leek for 8 minutes, until softened.

2. Turn the heat up to high, add the white wine and stock and bring to a boil.

3. Add the mussels and 2 tablespoons parsley. Stir the mussels around so they're coated with some of the liquid.

4. Turn the heat down so it is lightly simmering.

5. Place a tight-fitting lid on the top and steam the mussels for a couple of minutes until the mussels just pop open.

6. Transfer the mussels to the serving dishes.

7. Check the remaining liquid and season to taste. Pour it over the mussels and scatter the rest of the parsley on top.

8. Serve with lemon wedges.

# PISTACHIO SEARED TUNA

### INGREDIENTS

2 tsps olive oil

1 tbsp pistachios, finely chopped

½ tbsp pepper

½ tsp lemon zest

½ tsp red wine vinegar

1 tsp fresh rosemary, chopped

2 x 150g (5oz) tuna steaks

¼ cup (35g, 1¼ oz) green olives, pitted and sliced

### METHOD

1. Mix together in a small bowl the oil, pistachios, pepper, zest, vinegar and rosemary.

2. Rub the mix into the tuna steaks.

3. Heat a non-stick frying pan to high heat.

4. Fry the steaks for 1½ minutes on each side to sear them.

5. Remove from pan and slice into 1cm (½ in) thick slices.

6. Serve with fresh salad greens and olives sprinkled over.

# WASABI CRUSTED SALMON

## INGREDIENTS

200g (7oz) green beans, ends trimmed

1 punnet cherry tomatoes, halved

1 bunch broccolini, ends trimmed

2 tbsps olive oil

Salt and pepper, to taste

### Salmon

2 x 150g (5oz) salmon fillets, skin on

⅓ cup (40g, 1½ oz) roasted pistachios, finely chopped

⅓ cup (30g, 1oz) wasabi peas, finely chopped

2 tsps olive oil

Salt and pepper, to taste

## METHOD

1. Preheat oven to 190°C (375°F, Gas Mark 5). Line a baking tray with baking paper.

2. Toss the vegetables with the olive oil and season with salt and pepper. Place in the tray and set aside.

3. Line a deep baking tray with lightly oiled baking paper.

4. Place the salmon fillets in the tray.

5. Mix together the pistachios, peas and olive oil and season with salt and pepper.

6. Press the wasabi mixture into the top of the fillets (not the skin side).

7. Cover the tray with foil and bake the fillets for 20 minutes.

8. Remove foil and cook for another 10 minutes or until the salmon is cooked to your liking.

9. Bake the vegetables in a lower shelf in the oven for 30 minutes.

10. Serve the fillets on top of the vegetables.

# TANDOORI PRAWNS WITH BULGAR SALAD

## INGREDIENTS

### Prawns

300g (10oz) prawns, shelled and deveined

½ tsp turmeric

¼ tsp ginger, minced

¼ tsp garlic, crushed

½ tsp garam masala

2 tsps tandoori paste

2 tsps canola oil

### Salad

1 cup (180g, 6oz) bulgar

1 tbsp olive oil

1 medium onion, finely chopped

1 tsp ground oregano

2 tsps nigella seeds

½ tsp chilli flakes

2 cups (60g, 2oz) baby spinach

1 tsp lemon rind, finely grated

## METHOD

1. Pat the prawns dry with a paper towel.

2. Mix all the other ingredients for the prawns in a medium-size bowl so that they're thoroughly combined. Toss through the prawns so they're well coated.

3. Cover the container and put the prawns in the fridge for 4 hours to marinate.

4. Soak the bulgar in 3 cups of boiling water for 30 minutes. Drain and dry out on a tea towel.

5. While the bulgar is soaking heat the olive oil in a medium frying pan over medium heat. Fry the onion for 10 minutes until it is well browned. Add the oregano, nigella seeds, and chilli and fry for 1 minute.

6. Add the spinach and once it has softened, add the bulgar and lemon rind. Cook for 5 minutes on medium heat.

7. Season to taste.

8. To cook the prawns, heat a grill plate on high.

9. Grill the prawns for 2 minutes on each side until cooked and slightly charred on the outside.

10 Serve the prawns on top of the salad with lemon wedges on the side.

# GRILLED SEA BREAM

### INGREDIENTS

1 tbsp rosemary, roughly chopped

3 tbsps olive oil

1 large sea bream, scaled and cleaned

3 lemon slices, 5mm thick

1 tbsp lemon zest

1 tbsp lemon juice

2 tbsps black pepper

1 tbsp salt

Lemon wedges, to serve

### METHOD

1. Place the rosemary leaves in the olive and infuse for 15 minutes.

2. Pat the fish dry and cut 3 slashes into one side, 2cm (1in) deep. Poke the lemon slices into the slashes.

3. Mix together the oil, lemon zest, juice, pepper and salt.

4. Rub the mix over both sides of the fish.

5. Heat a grill pan to high heat.

6. Grill the bream for 8 minutes on each side, or until the fish is cooked through.

7. Serve with lemon wedges on the side.

# SALMON POKE

### INGREDIENTS

1 avocado

1 tsp lemon juice

Salt and pepper, to taste

200g (7oz) sashimi-grade fresh salmon fillets, no skin, deboned

1 tbsp soy sauce

2 tsps rice wine vinegar

1 tsp sesame oil

¼ tsp brown sugar

1 spring onion, sliced

1 cup (165g, 6oz) cooked black rice

1 Lebanese cucumber, peeled into ribbons

1 radish, sliced

½ tsp black sesame seeds

½ tsp white sesame seeds

1 sheet seaweed, finely chopped

### METHOD

1.  Mash the avocado with 1 teaspoon lemon juice and season with salt and pepper. Set aside.

2.  Lightly toast the sesame seeds for 1 minute in a small hot frying pan until just about to brown. Remove from pan immediately and set aside.

3.  Cut the salmon into 2cm (1in) cubes.

4.  Mix together in a medium bowl the soy sauce, vinegar, sesame oil and sugar. Stir the salmon through with half the spring onion. Cover and place in the refrigerator for at least 2 hours.

5.  Divide the rice between two serving bowls. Place the salmon, avocado, cucumber and radish on top.

6.  Sprinkle over the remaining spring onions as well as the sesame seeds and chopped seaweed.

# GLAZED SALMON WITH BROCCOLI MASH

## INGREDIENTS

### Mash

2 heads of broccoli, broken into florets

1 tsp salt

1 tbsp coconut oil

¼ cup (25g, 1oz) fresh ginger, thinly sliced

1 tsp coriander, chopped

1 tsp cayenne pepper

1 tsp fish sauce

### Salmon

½ cup (125ml, 4fl oz) soy sauce

2 tbsps lemon juice

¼ cup (80g, 3oz) maple syrup

3 garlic cloves, crushed

2 x 150g (5oz) salmon fillets

## METHOD

1. Boil the broccoli in salted water for 4 minutes until tender. Drain and place in a food processor.

2. Heat the coconut oil in a small frying pan over low heat and fry half the ginger for 2 minutes. Turn off heat.

3. Add the oil, without the ginger, to the broccoli as well as the coriander, pepper and fish sauce. Puree until smooth. Set aside.

4. Place the soy sauce, lemon juice, maple syrup, the rest of the ginger and the garlic in a small bowl and stir to combine.

5. Save 2 tablespoons of the marinade and pour the rest over the fillets and let them sit to marinate for 40 minutes in the refrigerator.

6. Heat a non-stick frying pan to medium-high heat.

7. Cook the salmon for 4 minutes on each side or until cooked to your liking.

8. Serve the salmon on top the broccoli mash and drizzle over the reserved marinade.

# THAI HOT FISH SOUP

## INGREDIENTS

2-3 small waxy potatoes, (such as kipfler) peeled and cut into 3cm (1in) cubes

1 tbsp canola oil

5 spring onions, chopped

⅓ cup (60g, 2oz) Thai green curry paste

1 green chilli, seeded and chopped

1 red chilli, finely chopped

1 garlic clove, crushed

2 tsps ginger, finely grated

¾ cup (200ml, 7fl oz) coconut milk

1⅔ cups (400ml, 13fl oz) fish stock

2 tbsps fish sauce

1 tbsp lime juice

1 tbsp brown sugar

200g (7oz) green beans, trimmed and cut into 4cm (1½ in) pieces

½ cup (60g, 2oz) cashews

1 cup (155g, 5oz) palm hearts, halved

3 white or purple baby eggplants, quartered

600g (1lb 5oz) white fish fillets (snapper or blue eye) cut into 3cm (1in) cubes

## METHOD

1. Boil potatoes for 8 minutes. Drain and set aside.

2. Heat oil in a large work over high heat.

3. Add the spring onion and fry for 2 minutes. Add the curry paste, chillies, garlic and ginger and fry for 1 minute.

4. Add the coconut milk and bring to the boil. Reduce heat and simmer for 3 minutes.

5. Add the stock, fish sauce, lime juice, sugar, beans, cashews, palm hearts and eggplants. Bring to the boil, then reduce heat and simmer for 10 minutes.

6. Add the potato and simmer for another 5 minutes.

7. Add the fish and simmer for 4 minutes or until the fish is cooked through.

# LEMON BAKED FISH

## INGREDIENTS

1 garlic clove, crushed

1 small lemon, zested and juiced, plus extra wedges to serve

1 tbsp Dijon mustard

3 tbsps flat-leaf parsley, roughly chopped

2 tbsps fresh oregano, roughly chopped

1 tbsp fresh basil, shredded

2 tsps olive oil

2 skinless, white fish fillets (such as snapper or bream), about 150g (5oz) each

## METHOD

1. Preheat oven to 230°C (445°F, Gas Mark 8) and line a baking dish with baking paper.

2. In a small bowl, mix together the garlic, lemon juice, mustard, 2 tablespoons parsley, oregano, basil and half the oil.

3. Place the fish in the baking tray and coat the top of each fillet with the herb mixture. Drizzle the rest of the lemon juice and oil over the top.

4. Bake for 10 minutes or until the fish is cooked through.

5. Serve with lemon wedges on the side.

# GRILLED FISH WITH BLACK RICE AND MANGO SALAD

## INGREDIENTS

1 medium sweet potato, peeled and cut into wedges

1 cup (135g, 5oz) butternut pumpkin, cubed

1 shallot, sliced

Olive oil, for baking

1 cup (225g, 8oz) black rice

2 tbsps orange juice

1 tbsp olive oil

1 tbsp lime juice

1 tsp chilli flakes

1 garlic clove, crushed

1 tsp fresh coriander, finely chopped

300g (10oz) white fish fillets (whiting or flathead)

1 mango, sliced

Salt and pepper, to taste

2 spring onions, chopped

## METHOD

1. Preheat the oven to 200°C (400°F, Gas Mark 6). Line a small baking tray with baking paper.

2. Toss the sweet potato, pumpkin and shallot lightly in olive oil and slide onto the baking tray. Transfer to the oven to bake for 30 minutes until tender. Set aside.

3. Cook rice according to packet instructions. Set aside to cool.

4. Mix the orange juice, 1 tablespoon of olive oil, lime juice, chilli, garlic and coriander together. Brush half of this sauce over the fish fillets.

5. Heat a grill pan to high heat. Grill the fish 4 minutes on each side.

6. In a large bowl, mix together the rice, baked vegetables, mango and the rest of the sauce.

7. Split the rice mix between the serving dishes and place the fish on top.

8. Garnish with spring onion.

# CAULIFLOWER ROSTI WITH SMOKED SALMON

## INGREDIENTS

### Salad

1 medium Lebanese cucumber, diced

1 small red onion, chopped

1 tbsp fresh dill, chopped

2 tbsps Greek yoghurt

2 tsps capers

Salt and pepper, to taste

1 tsp lemon juice

150g (5oz) smoked salmon

Lemon wedges, to serve

### Rosti

½ small head cauliflower

1 egg

1 spring onion, chopped

1 tsp chives, chopped

1 garlic clove, crushed

1 tbsp chickpea flour

2 tsps coconut oil

## METHOD

1. Toss all the salad ingredients except the salmon in a large bowl to thoroughly combine. Place in refrigerator until needed for serving.

2. Grate the cauliflower and mix together in a large bowl with the egg, onion, chives, garlic and chickpea flour. Add a pinch of salt and pepper.

3. Heat half the coconut oil over medium-high heat in a medium-sized non-stick frying pan.

4. Place half the cauliflower mix in the pan and press to flatten into a large circle, but take care to keep it thick enough so it doesn't break apart.

5. Cook for 5 minutes on each side or until golden brown.

6. Repeat with the rest of the mixture.

7. Serve the warm rostis with the salad mix on top and the smoked salmon on top of that.

8. Garnish with extra dill and lemon wedges on the side.

# TANGY GRILLED SALMON KEBABS

## INGREDIENTS

2 tbsps Dijon mustard

2-3 limes, cut into wedges, one half juiced

¼ tsp chilli flakes (or more to taste)

¼ tsp garlic, minced

¼ tsp cumin

Splash apple cider vinegar

12 skewers soaked in cold water for an hour

750g (1½ lb) salmon fillet cut into 2cm (1in) cubes

8-10 slices of prosciutto, cut into strips

Olive oil

½ tbsp black sesame seeds, crushed

½ tbsp white sesame seeds, crushed

## METHOD

1. Heat grill to medium.

2. Whisk together mustard, lime juice, chilli flakes, garlic, cumin, and vinegar in a small bowl and set aside.

3. Thread skewers, starting with a salmon cube, followed by a folded slice of prosciutto and then a lime wedge. Continue until the skewer is full, beginning and ending with salmon.

4. Brush with olive oil then liberally coat with spice mixture.

5. Sprinkle with crushed black and white sesame seeds.

6. Grill, turning from time to time until fish is opaque (about 5 minutes).

7. Serve immediately.

# EASY TOMATO AND BASIL FISH STEW

## INGREDIENTS

1 tbsp olive oil

1 medium onion, chopped

2 garlic cloves, crushed

1 tsp sweet paprika

1 tbsp tomato paste

1 tsp chilli flakes

1 x 400g (14oz) can chopped tomatoes

1 small red capsicum, chopped

½ cup (125ml, 4fl oz) dry white wine

2 cups (500ml, 1pt) fish or vegetable stock

½ tbsp flat-leaf parsley, chopped

500g (1lb 2oz) firm white fish fillets (such as Victoria perch or hake), cut into 4cm (1½ in) chunks

⅓ cup (15g, ½ oz) shredded basil

## METHOD

1. In a large pot, heat the olive oil over medium heat.

2. Add the onion and fry for 5 minutes. Add the garlic and fry for 1 minute.

3. Stir in the paprika, tomato paste and chilli and cook for a further minute.

4. Add the chopped tomatoes and capsicum and stir until bubbling.

5. Turn the heat to high and pour in the white wine. Once it is boiling, add the stock and again bring to the boil.

6. Turn the heat down to simmering and cook for 10 minutes.

7. Add the parsley, fish and half the basil.

8. Cover and simmer for 5-7 minutes until the fish is cooked.

9. Serve with a side salad and garnished with the rest of the basil.

# PRAWN CHOP SUEY

## INGREDIENTS

1 large egg

2 tbsps sesame oil

1 tsp cornflour

2 tbsps water

1 small onion, finely chopped

1 garlic clove, finely chopped

½ tbsp fresh ginger, minced

1 spring onion, sliced

1 medium carrot, cut into matchsticks

200g (7oz) prawns, deveined and peeled

1 tsp oyster sauce

Salt and pepper

2 cups (330g, 12oz) cooked long-grain brown rice

1 tbsp chives, chopped

1 tbsp soy sauce

## METHOD

1. Whisk the egg in a small bowl for 1 minute until light and fluffy.

2. In a medium wok, heat 2 tsps sesame oil over medium heat. Pour the egg in and spread out into a thin omelette. Cook for 2 minutes on each side.

3. Remove from the wok and cut into thin 2cm (1in) slices. Set aside.

4. Wipe the wok down and add the rest of the sesame oil. Heat to high heat.

5. Mix together the cornflour and water and set aside.

6. Fry the onion, garlic, ginger and half the spring onion for 1 minute.

7. Add the carrot and prawns and cook for 1 minute, stirring all the time.

8. Add 4 tablespoons of water. When it starts to boil, add the oyster sauce, some grinds of salt and pepper and the cornflour mixture. Stir through quickly.

9. Add the rice, egg and chives and stir to combine and heat through. Add soy sauce to taste.

10. Serve garnished with the remaining spring onions.

# POULTRY

# CHICKEN PESTO SALAD

### INGREDIENTS

**Pesto**

2½ cups (80g, ¾ oz) fresh basil leaves

½ cup (70g, 2½ oz) pine nuts

¾ cup (75g, 3oz) Parmesan cheese, grated

Salt and pepper, to taste

⅓ cup (80ml, 3fl oz) olive oil

600g (1lb 5oz) cooked chicken breasts, cut into small strips

1 punnet cherry tomatoes, halved

¾ cup (40g, 1½ oz) semi-sun-dried tomatoes, halved

500g (1lb 2oz) baby spinach leaves

300g (10oz) feta, cubed

### METHOD

1. Place basil leaves and pine nuts in a food processer with Parmesan and salt and pepper to taste.

2. Add oil gradually, until the pesto forms a smooth paste.

3. Toss together the chicken, tomatoes, semi-sun-dried tomatoes, spinach leaves and feta in a large serving bowl with pesto to taste.

# RICOTTA STUFFED CHICKEN

## INGREDIENTS

2 x 150g (5oz) chicken breasts

300g (10oz) ricotta (fresh, not in a tub)

½ cup (60g, 2oz) Parmesan cheese, grated

2 cups (60g, 2oz) baby spinach, chopped

1 egg

1 tbsp flat-leaf parsley, roughly chopped

Salt and pepper, to taste

¾ cup (200ml, 7fl oz) chicken stock

## METHOD

1. Preheat the oven to 200°C (400°F, Gas Mark 6).

2. Pat dry the chicken breasts. Cut slices from the top down into the breasts, about 1½ cm (¾ in) apart, that stop 1cm (½ in) from the bottom.

3. In a medium bowl, mix together the ricotta, half of the Parmesan, the baby spinach, egg, parsley and a good couple of grinds of salt and pepper.

4. Stuff the ricotta mixture in between the slices in the breasts. Divide the mixture evenly between the two breasts.

5. Place the breasts into a baking dish that will hold them snugly.

6. Gently pour over the stock and sprinkle the rest of the Parmesan over the top.

7. Bake in the oven, uncovered, for 30 minutes or until the breasts are completely cooked through.

8. Serve warm with a side of salad.

SERVES 2 ★ PREP 10MIN ★ COOK TIME 20MIN

# SPICY COCONUT CHICKEN

### INGREDIENTS

⅓ cup (100ml, 3½ fl oz) coconut milk

⅓ cup (100ml, 3½ fl oz) coconut cream

2 cups (500ml, 1pt) chicken stock

2 tbsps lime juice

2 tsps fish sauce

1 green chilli, seeded and finely chopped

1 tsp chilli sauce

2 tbsps fresh basil, shredded

500g (1lb 2oz) chicken breast, cut into 3cm (1in) cubes

Salt and pepper, to taste

Lemon wedges, to serve

### METHOD

1. Heat the coconut milk, cream, stock, lime juice, fish sauce, chilli and chilli sauce in a large pot until boiling.
2. Reduce the heat to a simmer, add half the basil and the chicken. Cover and simmer for 15 minutes.
3. Adjust taste with salt and pepper.
4. Serve with lemon wedges and garnished with the rest of the basil.

# MUSTARD CHICKEN SKEWERS

## INGREDIENTS

1 tbsp apple cider vinegar

2 tbsps Dijon mustard

3 tbsps seeded mustard

300g (10oz) chicken breast fillets, cut into 3cm (1in) cubes

2 tbsps olive oil

¼ tsp salt

¼ tsp pepper

1 garlic clove, crushed

Lemon wedges, to serve

Sprig parsley, to garnish

## METHOD

1. Combine the vinegar, 1 tablespoon of Dijon and one tablespoon of seeded mustard together and coat the chicken pieces with it. Cover the chicken and place in the refrigerator for at least 2 hours.

2. Soak wooden skewers in hot water for 30 minutes before use.

3. Mix together the oil, salt and pepper, garlic and the rest of the mustards in a small bowl.

4. Thread the chicken pieces onto the skewers.

5. Heat a grill plate on high heat.

6. Place the skewers on the grill and brush with the mustard oil.

7. Grill for 2 minutes on all four sides, brushing each time with the oil.

8. Serve hot with lemon wedges and garnished with parsley.

# CREAMY CHICKEN SALAD

## INGREDIENTS

¾ cup (185ml, 6fl oz) Greek yoghurt

¼ tsp salt

1 tbsp fresh mint, finely chopped

½ tsp lemon juice

300g (10oz) cooked chicken breast, cubed

½ cup (90g/3oz) seedless black grapes, halved

1 cup (100g, 3½ oz) celery, sliced

2 spring onions, sliced

Salt and pepper, to taste

2 tbsps flat-leaf parsley, roughly chopped, to garnish

## METHOD

1. Mix together the yoghurt, salt, mint and lemon juice in a medium-sized bowl.

2. Stir the cubed chicken through the yoghurt.

3. Cover and place in the refrigerator for at least 30 minutes.

4. In a large serving bowl, mix together the chicken, any remaining yoghurt mix and the rest of the ingredients.

5. Season to taste with salt and pepper.

6. Serve garnished with parsley

# MEDITERRANEAN ROAST CHICKEN AND VEGETABLES

## INGREDIENTS

2 small zucchinis,
sliced

2 medium sweet
potatoes, cut into wedges

1 head of garlic, cut in
half crossways

1 small red onion,
cut into wedges

3 tbsps olive oil

2 tsps fresh rosemary,
finely chopped

2 tsps fresh oregano,
finely chopped

Salt and pepper, to taste

4 chicken Marylands,
skin on

2 vines of cherry
tomatoes (about 12
tomatoes in total)

## METHOD

1.  Preheat the oven to 200°C (400°F, Gas Mark 6).

2.  In a large bowl, gently toss the zucchini, sweet potato, garlic head halves and onion with 1 tablespoon olive oil, half the rosemary, half the oregano and a good couple of grinds of salt and pepper.

3.  Brush the chicken pieces with the remaining olive oil, herbs and some more salt and pepper.

4.  Arrange the chicken pieces and all the vegetables, except the tomatoes, in a large baking dish.

5.  Place in the oven and bake for 35 minutes.

6.  Add the tomatoes and bake for a further 20 minutes.

7.  Serve each Maryland with an equal portion of baked vegetables.

# CHICKEN SALAD BOWL WITH CREAMY TAHINI SAUCE

## INGREDIENTS

1 medium carrot,
cut into thin strips.

1 small zucchini,
cut into matchsticks

½ tsp black sesame
seeds

1 tsp white sesame seeds

300g (10oz) cooked
chicken breast, shredded

Salt and pepper

½ red cabbage, shredded

3 radishes, halved and
thinly sliced

1 small red capsicum,
deseeded and sliced

¼ cup (5g, ¼ oz) micro
greens, loosely packed

### Tahini dressing

1 x 400g (14oz) can
chickpeas, drained, rinsed

2 garlic cloves, crushed

½ cup (125ml, 4fl oz)
olive oil

3 tbsps tahini

¼ cup (60ml, 2fl oz)
Greek yoghurt

3 tbsps lemon juice

1 tsp cumin

¼ tsp cayenne

## METHOD

1. Blanch the carrots and zucchini by boiling them for 1 minute then plunging them in cold water.

2. Mix the sesame seeds through the cooked chicken and add a grind of salt and pepper.

3. Divide all the salad ingredients and the chicken between two serving bowls and sprinkle over the micro greens.

4. To make the sauce, place all the ingredients into a blender and puree until smooth and creamy.

5. Season to taste with salt and pepper.

6. Serve the sauce on the side of the chicken and vegetable bowl as a dipping sauce.

# CHICKEN AND BROCCOLI BROTH

## INGREDIENTS

2 tsps sesame oil

2 spring onions, sliced

1 tbsp fresh ginger, minced

1 large red chilli, seeded and chopped

1 lemongrass stalk, trimmed, white part only, crushed with a heavy mallet

½ tsp brown sugar

4 cups (1L, 2pt) chicken stock

1 tsp fish sauce

1 head broccoli, broken into florets

600g (1lb 5oz) chicken fillets, cut into 1cm (½ in) slices

2 tsps fresh lime juice

250g (9oz) vermicelli rice noodles (omit these if following a strict no-carb diet)

Salt and pepper, to taste

## METHOD

1. Heat the oil in a large soup pot over medium heat. Fry the spring onions and ginger for 1 minute.

2. Add the chilli, lemongrass and sugar and fry for a further minute.

3. Add the stock, fish sauce, broccoli, chicken and half the lime juice and bring to a boil. Reduce heat to a simmer, cover and cook for 15 minutes.

4. Remove the lemongrass stalks and add the noodles, if using, to the soup. Simmer for 3 more minutes.

5. Adjust the soup to taste with the rest of the lime juice and salt and pepper.

6. Serve hot.

# CHICKEN AND PRUNE STEW

## INGREDIENTS

2 tbsps coconut oil

2 medium onions, chopped

2 tsps cumin

½ tsp cinnamon

1kg (2lb) chicken pieces, skin off

2 cups (300g, 10oz) prunes

2 carrots, chopped

1 tomato, chopped

1 cup (125g, 4oz) almonds, halved

2 tsps lemon zest

2 cups (500ml, 1pt) chicken stock

¼ cup (10g, ¼ oz) flat-leaf parsley, roughly chopped

¼ cup (30g, 1oz) flaked almonds to garnish

## METHOD

1. Preheat the oven to 180°C (350°F, Gas Mark 4).

2. Heat the oil in a large oven-proof dish over medium heat.

3. Fry the onion for 4 minutes until softened. Add the cumin and cinnamon and stir for 1 minute.

4. Add the chicken pieces and cook for 3 minutes on each side until lightly browned.

5. Add the prunes, carrots, tomato, almond halves and half the lemon zest.

6. Stir to distribute the ingredients evenly and cook for 5 minutes. Pour the chicken stock over the top.

7. Place in the oven and bake for 40 minutes.

8. Remove from the oven and serve warm garnished with parsley and flaked almonds.

# CRUNCHY QUINOA SALAD

## INGREDIENTS

1¼ cups (210g, 8oz) yellow quinoa

½ tsp turmeric

300g (10oz) green beans

4 radishes, halved and sliced

1 large yellow capsicum, sliced

¼ small red cabbage, shredded

400g (14oz) cooked chicken breast, shredded

4 cups (120g, 4oz) baby spinach

½ cup (20g, ¾ oz) flat-leaf parsley, roughly chopped

1 cup (45g, 1½ oz) micro greens

Salt and pepper, to taste

1½ tbsps olive oil

## METHOD

1. Rinse quinoa in cold water. Pour into a medium-sized pot with 2 cups cold water and the turmeric. Bring to a boil. Reduce heat and simmer, covered, for 15 minutes. Drain and set aside.

2. Boil the beans for 2 minutes then rinse under cold water so they're still crunchy.

3. Toss all the ingredients together in a salad bowl with salt and pepper and drizzle olive oil over the top.

**SERVES 4 ★ PREP 15MIN ★ COOK TIME 1HR**

# MOROCCAN CHICKEN TAJINE

### INGREDIENTS

2 tbsps olive oil

600g (1lb 5oz) chicken breasts, cubed

1 onion, finely chopped

3 garlic cloves, crushed

2 tbsps ginger, minced

½ tsp ground cinnamon

2 tsps ground cumin

1 tsp nigella seeds

2 tsps ground coriander

½ tsp cayenne pepper

600g (1lb 5oz) butternut pumpkin, cubed

½ cup (80g, 3oz) dried cranberries

¼ cup (50g, 2oz) preserved lemon, diced

2 cups (500ml, 1pt) chicken stock

1½ tbsps honey

Salt and pepper, to taste

¼ cup (60g, 2oz) Greek feta, crumbled

½ cup (10g, ¼ oz) loosely packed mint leaves

¼ lemon, zested in thin strips

### METHOD

1. Preheat the oven to 180°C (350°F, Gas Mark 4).

2. Heat the oil in a large oven-proof casserole dish over medium-high heat. Fry the chicken for 5 minutes, until browned on the outside, then remove from the dish and set aside.

3. Reduce heat to medium. Add the onions and more oil if needed. Cook the onion for 5 minutes until softened and golden. Add the garlic and ginger and cook for 30 seconds. Add the spices and cook for 1 minute until fragrant.

4. Add the pumpkin, cranberries and preserved lemon and cook for 1 minute.

5. Add the stock, chicken and honey and stir to mix through.

6. Place in the oven, covered, and bake for 45 minutes.

7. Season to taste.

8. Serve garnished with feta, mint leaves and lemon zest.

# THAI CHICKEN SALAD

## INGREDIENTS

2 x 150g (5oz) chicken breasts

3 tbsps fish sauce

4 garlic cloves, crushed

2 tbsps palm sugar

½ tsp white pepper

2 tbsps soy sauce

2 tbsps lime juice

2 tbsps peanut oil

**Salad**

150g (5oz) soba noodles

¼ red cabbage, shredded

1 large Lebanese cucumber, cut into 1cm (½ in) cubes

## METHOD

1. Slice the chicken breasts into 1cm (½ in) thick slices. Place in a bowl.

2. Mix together in a small bowl the fish sauce, garlic, sugar, pepper, soy sauce, lime juice and 1 tablespoon peanut oil.

3. Reserve half the sauce and toss the rest with the slices of chicken. Cover the bowl and place the chicken in the refrigerator for at least 2 hours.

4. Cook the noodles according to the packet instructions. Once al dente, rinse under cold water.

5. Toss together the noodles, cabbage and cucumber with the reserved sauce and set aside.

6. Heat a medium-sized frying pan to medium-high heat. Add the sliced chicken and cook for 10 minutes, turning the pieces once, until the chicken is browned.

7. Serve the chicken slices on top of the noodle salad.

# DUCK SALAD

## INGREDIENTS

4 tbsps brown sugar

4 tsps balsamic vinegar

1 firm buerre bosc pear, cored and cut into wedges (use a different variety of pear if it's easier)

2 duck breasts

2 cups (60g, 2oz) baby spinach

50g (2oz) shaved Parmesan sheets

## METHOD

1.  Place the brown sugar in a small non-stick frying pan and gently heat to melt the sugar until it is almost bubbling. Take off the heat and stir in the vinegar until it becomes a sticky syrup.

2.  Return to medium heat and place the pear slices in the pan. Cook on each side for 4 minutes or until brown and caramelised. Remove from the heat and set aside.

3.  Heat a medium frying pan to low heat and place the two duck breasts skin down. Then cook for 20 minutes until the skin is browned and crisp. Turn over and cook on the flesh side for 5 minutes.

4.  Remove from duck from the pan, let sit for 5 minutes then cut into slices.

5.  Layer a quarter of the spinach on each dish, then some pear slices, then the Parmesan, followed by the rest of the spinach, then the duck and top with the remaining pear.

6.  Drizzle with leftover sauce from cooking the pears.

SERVES 2 ★ PREP 15MIN ★ COOK TIME 25MIN

# CHICKEN ORANGE SALAD

## INGREDIENTS

1 bunch asparagus, trimmed

1 orange, sliced

1 tbsp olive oil

1 tsp lemon juice

Salt and pepper, to taste

300g (10oz) chicken breast

½ tsp dried basil

1 cup (20g, 2oz) watercress

1 tsp olive oil, to garnish

## METHOD

1. To grill the vegetables, toss the asparagus in the olive oil and the lemon juice and a good grind of salt and pepper.

2. Heat a grill plate on high and grill asparagus for 4 minutes on each side until they are slightly charred on each side. Set aside.

3. Coat the chicken fillets in the rest of the oil and the basil.

4. Place on the grill and cook for 7 minutes on each side until cooked all the way through.

5. Remove from the grill and cut into 5mm (¼ in) thick slices.

6. Toss the chicken, vegetables and salad leaves together in a salad bowl.

7. Serve drizzled with olive oil.

# GRILLED CHICKEN AND QUINOA SALAD

## INGREDIENTS

¾ cup (120g, 4oz) quinoa

3 tbsps olive oil

300g (10oz) chicken breast

½ tsp cumin

½ tsp ground coriander

½ tsp salt

½ tsp pepper

1 small onion, halved and sliced

2 baby eggplants, halved lengthways and sliced

10 cherry tomatoes, halved

¼ cup (10g, ¼ oz) basil leaves, shredded

## METHOD

1. Rinse quinoa in cold water. Pour into a medium-sized pot with 2 cups cold water, 1 tablespoon oil and a dash of salt. Bring to a boil. Reduce heat and simmer, covered, for 15 minutes. Drain and set aside.

2. Season the chicken breasts with the cumin, coriander and salt and pepper.

3. Heat 1 tablespoon oil in a medium frying pan over medium-high heat.

4. Fry the chicken for 6 minutes each side until cooked through. Set aside.

5. Heat the rest of the oil in the pan and fry the onion for 5 minutes until softened. Add the eggplant and fry for 8 minutes until softened, turning as needed.

6. Remove from pan.

7. To assemble the salad, slice the chicken into 1cm (½ in) thick slices and toss with the eggplant, onion, tomatoes and quinoa.

8. Season to taste and garnish with the shredded basil.

# TURMERIC CHICKEN WITH PUMPKIN SALAD

## INGREDIENTS

1 garlic clove, crushed

1 tsp lemon zest

¼ tsp turmeric

½ tbsp plus 2 tsps olive oil

2 x 150g (5oz) chicken breasts

400g (14oz) butternut pumpkin, cubed

Salt and pepper, to taste

3 cups (90g, 3oz) salad leaves

1 tsp balsamic vinegar

2 tsps white sesame seeds

2 tsps black sesame seeds

2 lime wedges, to serve

## METHOD

1. Preheat the oven to 230°C (445°F, Gas Mark 8).

2. Mix the garlic, lemon zest, turmeric and ½ tablespoon olive together in a small bowl. Coat the chicken in the mixture and place in a baking dish. Set aside.

3. Lightly toss the pumpkin with 1 teaspoon olive oil and salt and pepper and place in the baking dish with the chicken.

4. Bake in the oven for 10 minutes.

5. Reduce the heat in the oven to 180°C (350°F, Gas Mark 4) and bake for a further 20 minutes until the pumpkin is tender and the chicken is cooked through.

6. Divide salad leaves between two serving plates.

7. Place the pumpkin on top and drizzle over the balsamic vinegar and season to taste.

8. Add the chicken to the dish and garnish with the sesame seeds and a wedge of lime.

SERVES 4 ★ PREP 15MIN ★ COOK TIME 40MIN

# NOURISHING CHICKEN SOUP

## INGREDIENTS

2 tbsps olive oil

2 medium onions, diced

½ tbsp tomato paste

1 tsp sweet paprika

3 medium carrots, halved lengthways and sliced

½ cup (50g, 2oz) celery, chopped

6 cups (1.5L, 50fl oz) chicken stock

½ tbsps Worcestershire sauce

¼ head white cabbage, sliced and chopped

2 cups (60g, 2oz) fresh spinach, chopped

400g (14oz) chicken breasts, cooked and shredded

Salt and pepper, to taste

3 spring onions, sliced

## METHOD

1. In a large pot, heat the olive oil over medium-high heat.

2. Fry the onions for 6 minutes, until softened and slightly browned.

3. Stir in the tomato paste and paprika and cook for 1 minute.

4. Add the carrots and celery and cook for a further 3 minutes.

5. Turn the heat up to high and add the stock and Worcestershire sauce.

6. Add the cabbage, bring to a boil, then reduce the heat and simmer, covered, for 30 minutes.

7. Add the spinach and chicken and cook for a further 5 minutes, until the chicken is heated through.

8. Season to taste with salt and pepper.

9. Serve garnished with spring onions.

# TURKEY BOATS

## INGREDIENTS

1 avocado

½ tsp lemon juice

1 tsp Greek yoghurt

Salt and pepper, to taste

2 tsps coconut oil

1 small onion, finely chopped

1 garlic clove, crushed

¼ tsp salt

½ tsp chilli powder

½ tsp cumin

½ tsp ground oregano

300g (10oz) turkey mince

2 radicchios, rinsed, leaves separated

## METHOD

1. Mash the avocado with the lemon juice and yoghurt. Season to taste with salt and pepper.

2. Heat the oil in a medium-sized frying pan over medium heat.

3. Fry the onion and garlic for 5 minutes, add the salt, chilli, cumin and oregano and cook for a further minute.

4. Add the turkey and fry for 6 minutes or until browned.

5. Place a large spoonful of turkey mince in each radicchio leaf and top with avocado mix.

# SESAME CHICKEN BOWL

## INGREDIENTS

1½ tbsps sesame oil

1½ tbsps rice wine vinegar

150g (5oz) buckwheat noodles

1½ tbsps soy sauce

1 tbsp brown sugar

3 tbsps warm water

2 x 150g (5oz) chicken breasts

1 small red capsicum, sliced

1 small carrot, cut into matchsticks

1 small red onion, halved and thinly sliced

1 tsp sesame seeds

## METHOD

1.  Whisk together half a tablespoon of sesame oil and half a tablespoon of rice vinegar in a small bowl.

2.  Boil the noodles according to instructions. After draining, toss them with the sesame oil and vinegar mix. Set aside.

3.  Mix together the rest of the sesame oil, vinegar, soy sauce, brown sugar and warm water in another small bowl.

4.  Coat the chicken with half the sauce.

5.  Heat a wok to medium heat and add a teaspoon of the sauce.

6.  Add the chicken breasts and cook for 5 minutes on each side, or until the breasts are cooked through. Set the chicken aside for 5 minutes, covered, to rest.

7.  Reduce the heat to medium. Fry the capsicum, carrot and onion for 2 minutes, stirring the whole time. Remove the pan from the heat.

8.  Slice the chicken into thick strips.

9.  Serve the vegetables and chicken on top of the noodles.

10. Pour over remaining sauce and garnish with sesame seeds.

# CONFIT DUCK WITH MUSHROOM SAUCE

## INGREDIENTS

2 tbsps salt

3 garlic cloves, crushed

2 tsps orange zest

1 tbsp thyme, finely chopped

2 tbsps sage, finely chopped

Pepper. to taste

2 duck Marylands, skin on

2 cups (430g, 15oz) duck fat

1½ tbsps unsalted butter

1 garlic clove, crushed

3 shallots, sliced

200g (7oz) button mushrooms, halved and sliced

200g (7oz) small oyster mushrooms, halved and sliced

½ tsp cornflour

½ cup (125ml, 4fl oz) vegetable stock

1 tbsp flat-leaf parsley, roughly chopped, to garnish

Sprig rosemary, to garnish

## METHOD

1. Mix together the salt, garlic, zest, thyme, sage and a couple of grinds of pepper. Reserve 1 teaspoon of this salt mix.

2. Sprinkle a third of the salt mix in the bottom of a baking dish. Coat the duck legs thoroughly in the rest of the salt mixture and place them skin-side down in the baking dish. Cover and refrigerate for at least 24 hours to draw out as much moisture as you can.

3. Preheat oven to 150°C (300°F, Gas Mark 2).

4. Remove the duck from the refrigerator and rinse off the salt mixture. Pat dry.

5. Place the duck legs snugly in a baking dish. Melt the duck fat and stir in the reserved salt mix.

6. Pour the fat over the duck legs and bake in the oven for 4 hours until the meat is nearly falling off the bone. Just before serving, place the duck skin up under a hot grill for 4 minutes to crisp the skin.

7. To make the mushroom sauce, melt the butter in a medium-sized frying pan over medium heat. Add the garlic and shallots and fry for 3 minutes. Add the mushrooms and fry for 6 minutes until browned.

8. Stir the cornflour into the stock and pour over the mushrooms. Stir until the sauce has thickened slightly.

9. Season to taste with salt and pepper. Serve garnished with parsley and rosemary.

# LOW-FAT MINI TURKEY BURGERS

## INGREDIENTS

500g (1lb 2oz) turkey mince

½ cup (125g, 4oz) feta cheese, crumbled

1 red onion, finely chopped

1 tbsp parsley, chopped

1 tbsp mint, chopped

1 tbsp milk

½ tsp salt

⅛ tsp black pepper

Olive oil, for frying

## METHOD

1. In a large bowl combine turkey, feta, onion, parsley, mint, milk, salt, and pepper. Using your hands, mix until thoroughly combined.

2. Evenly divide the mixture and shape into 8 balls. Press each ball flat with hands to form 8 small patties.

3. Heat oil in a large frying pan over medium heat.

4. Cook each pattie for 3-4 minutes on each side, until golden brown and turkey is cooked through.

# ROAST CHICKEN BREAST WITH SWEET CHILLI SAUCE

## INGREDIENTS

2 x 150g (5oz) chicken breasts

1 tsp olive oil

¼ tsp Chinese five-spice mix

### Sauce

¼ cup (60ml, 2fl oz) soy sauce

2 tbsps brown sugar

2 tbsps sweet chilli sauce

2 tbsps apple cider vinegar

¼ tsp salt

Pinch of pepper

1 garlic clove, minced

¼ tsp fresh ginger, minced

1 tsp cornflour

¼ tsp chilli powder

1 tsp fresh lemon thyme, to garnish

## METHOD

1. Place all the sauce ingredients together in a bowl and mix thoroughly. Set aside

2. Coat the chicken in the oil and five-spice mix.

3. Heat a grill pan to medium-high heat. Grill the chicken breasts for 6 minutes on each side or until thoroughly cooked through. Remove from pan and let sit while you cook the sauce.

4. Heat the sauce mix in a small pot until almost at a simmer and thickened, stirring the whole time. Remove from heat once thickened.

5. Slice the chicken into 2cm (1in) thick slices.

6. Top with the sauce and garnish with thyme leaves.

7. Serve with a side of roasted vegetables or fresh salad.

# CITRUS CHICKEN WITH ROASTED CAULIFLOWER

## INGREDIENTS

1 medium head cauliflower, broken into florets

2 tsps caraway seeds

2 tsps ground cumin

2 tbsps olive oil

Salt and pepper

2 tbsps butter

4 garlic cloves, crushed

1 tbsp lemon juice

2 tsps lemon zest

1 tbsp orange juice

2 tsps orange zest

4 x 150g (5oz) chicken breasts

¼ cup (10g, ¼ oz) flat-leaf parsley, roughly chopped

1 small orange, sliced

## METHOD

1.  Preheat the oven to 230°C (445°F, Gas Mark 8) and line a large flat baking tray with baking paper.

2.  Toss the cauliflower with the caraway seeds, cumin and olive oil. Season with salt and pepper. Bake in the oven for 35 minutes or until the cauliflower is tender and browned.

3.  While the cauliflower is baking, melt the butter and whisk in the garlic, juices, zests and a teaspoon each of salt and pepper.

4.  Pour the melted butter mixture into a separate baking dish and lay the chicken breasts on top. Brush some of the butter mixture over the tops of the breasts.

5.  Place the dish in the oven and bake for 5 minutes.

6.  Remove the chicken and brush over the butter mix.

7.  Bake the chicken for a further 10 minutes, then remove and brush again with the butter mixture.

8.  Return the chicken to the oven and bake for another 10 minutes until the chicken is completely cooked through.

9.  Remove from oven and let sit for 5 minutes.

10. Serve the chicken with the roasted cauliflower, seasoned to taste and garnished with parsley and slices of orange.

# GREEN CHICKEN CURRY

## INGREDIENTS

1 cup (250ml, 8fl oz) coconut milk

2 tbsps green Thai curry paste

400g (14oz) chicken thigh fillets, cut into 4cm (1½ in) pieces

7 Thai eggplants, quartered

2 cups (500ml, 1pt) water

150g (5oz) green beans, cut into 4cm (1½ in) pieces

⅓ cup (60g, 2oz) pea eggplants

2 spring onions, sliced

2 tbsps fish sauce

4 kaffir lime leaves

1 tbsp brown sugar

1 red chilli, sliced

½ cup (10g, ¼ oz) loosely packed Thai basil leaves

## METHOD

1. Pour half the coconut milk into a medium-sized pot and add the curry paste. Heat over medium heat for 4 minutes, stirring the whole time.

2. Add the chicken pieces and stir for 5 minutes. Add the Thai eggplants, the rest of the coconut milk and 1 cup water.

3. Let the chicken simmer for 10 minutes, then add the beans, pea eggplants, half the spring onions, fish sauce, lime leaves, sugar and chilli.

4. Let it boil quickly for 1 minute.

5. Remove from heat, stir in the basil leaves and serve.

# CHICKEN PHO

### INGREDIENTS

3 cups (750ml, 24fl oz) chicken stock

1 tsp ginger, finely chopped

1 garlic clove, crushed

1 star anise

300g (10oz) cooked chicken, sliced

1 tsp fish sauce

1 lime, cut into wedges

Salt and pepper, to taste

150g (5oz) vermicelli rice noodles, cooked according to packet directions

½ cup (10g, ¼ oz) coriander leaves

150g (5oz) beanshoots

1 long red chilli, sliced

Sweet chilli sauce, to serve

### METHOD

1.  Simmer the stock with the ginger, garlic and star anise for at least 40 minutes.

2.  Add the chicken, fish sauce and the juice of two lime wedges and cook for a further 5 minutes.

3.  Season to taste with salt and pepper.

4.  Serve poured over the noodles, and garnish with beanshoots, coriander, chilli slices and remaining lime wedges.

5.  Add a dash of sweet chilli sauce to give it an extra kick.

# CHICKEN AND ROCKET PIZZA

## INGREDIENTS

### Crust

1 medium head cauliflower

¼ cup (25g, 1oz) Parmesan, grated

¼ cup (30g, 1oz) mozzarella, grated

Pinch of salt

1½ tsps mixed herbs

1 egg

Olive oil spray

### Topping

2 tbsps tomato paste

1 tsp water

½ cup (60g, 2oz) pizza cheese

50g (2oz) oyster mushrooms, sliced

150g (5oz) cooked chicken, shredded

200g (7oz) rocket

6 cherry tomatoes, halved

## METHOD

1. Preheat the oven to 230°C (445°F, Gas Mark 8) and place a large flat baking tray in the oven to heat up. (Use a pizza stone if you have one.)

2. Break off the florets of cauliflower and place in a blender. Pulse until you have broken it down into breadcrumb-size pieces. You need at least 3 cups of cauliflower crumbs.

3. Place cauliflower into a microwave-proof bowl and heat on high in the microwave for 4 minutes. Dry out on a tea towel, then use the tea towel to wring as much liquid as you can out of the cauliflower crumbs.

4. Mix together thoroughly the crumbs, Parmesan, mozzarella, salt, 1 teaspoon herbs and egg.

5. Spray some baking paper with olive oil. Pat the mixture down onto some baking paper to form a 30cm (12in) pizza base. Slide the baking paper onto the baking tray and bake in the oven for 9 minutes, until it starts to lightly brown on the top.

6. Remove from the oven.

7. Mix together the tomato paste, water and rest of the herbs in a small bowl.

8. Spread the tomato mixture over the base.

9. Top with the cheese, then with the mushrooms and chicken.

10. Sprinkle over the rocket and tomato halves.

11. Bake in the oven for 12 minutes or until the pizza is starting to brown at the edges.

12. Remove from oven, let it cool for 5 minutes before serving.

# BEEF, LAMB AND PORK

# MEDITERRANEAN ROAST LAMB SHOULDER

## INGREDIENTS

4 tbsps olive oil

½ tbsp ground cumin

2 tsps dried oregano

2 sprigs rosemary,
1 sprig finely chopped

4 garlic cloves, crushed

Salt and pepper

5 baby eggplants, halved
lengthways

4 small parsnips

5 long sweet yellow
capsicums

12 baby carrots

1 x 1.4kg (3lb) lamb
shoulder

500g (1lb 2oz) Greek feta

1 cup (140g, 5oz)
Kalamata olives

1 tbsp sumac

## METHOD

1. Preheat the oven to 150°C (300°F, Gas Mark 2).

2. In a small bowl, mix together half the olive oil, cumin, oregano, chopped rosemary, garlic and 1 teaspoon each of pepper and salt.

3. Cut the eggplants into quarters, halve the parsnips and trim the ends of the carrots. Cover and set aside.

4. Coat the lamb with the oil and herb mixture, then place in a large baking dish.

5. Place the dish in the oven, along with a small bowl of water. Bake for 3 hours. Top up the bowl with water as needed.

6. Toss the prepared vegetables and yellow capsicum with half the remaining olive oil and give a good couple of grinds of salt and pepper.

7. Place in the baking dish with the lamb and return to the oven and bake for another hour. Remove the lamb and let it sit, covered.

8. Turn the heat up to 200°C (400°F, Gas Mark 6) for 15 minutes.

9. Serve the lamb with the roasted vegetables and feta and olives.

10. Drizzle remaining olive oil over and add a sprinkle of sumac over the top to garnish.

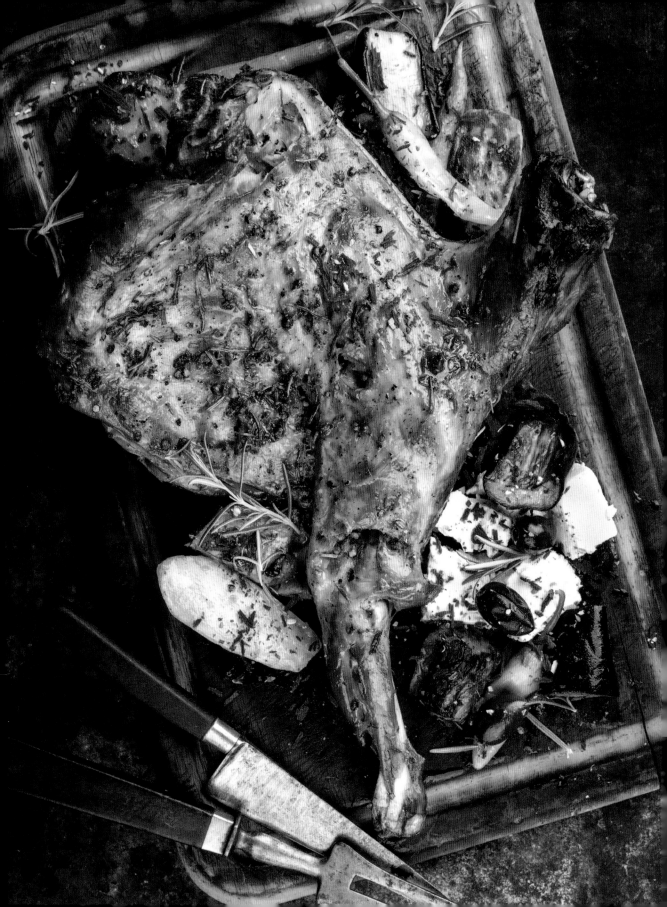

# STEAK WITH BRUSSELS SPROUTS AND RED WINE JUS

## INGREDIENTS

12 Brussels sprouts, halved

1 tbsp coconut oil, melted

½ tsp Dijon mustard

½ tsp salt

1½ cups (270g, 9oz) red seedless grapes

1 tsp butter

2 x 150g (5oz) sirloin steaks

### Jus

1 cup (250ml, 8fl oz) beef stock

½ cup (125ml, 4fl oz) red wine

½ tsp thyme leaves, finely chopped

1 garlic clove, crushed

1 square 70% cocoa dark chocolate

Salt and pepper, to taste

## METHOD

1. Preheat the oven to 180°C (350°F, Gas Mark 4).

2. In a small baking dish, toss together the Brussels sprouts, oil, mustard and salt.

3. Place in the oven and bake for 20 minutes.

4. Add the grapes, mix through and bake for a further 15 minutes, or until the sprouts start to brown.

5. While the vegetables are baking, prepare the steak and jus.

6. To cook the steaks, heat the butter in a heavy-based medium frying pan over high heat.

7. Add the steaks and fry for 4 minutes on each side until medium rare.

8. Let steak sit, covered, for at least 5 minutes.

9. To make the jus, heat the stock, wine, thyme and garlic in the same pan that you cooked the sirloin in.

10. Bring to a boil, then reduce to a simmer and cook for about 20 minutes more until the liquid is reduced by just under half.

11. Remove from the heat and stir in the chocolate.

12. Serve the steak with the roasted vegetables and pour the jus over the top.

13. Season with salt and pepper to taste.

# LENTIL AND SAUSAGE SOUP

## INGREDIENTS

1 tbsp olive oil

1 medium brown onion, finely chopped

2 garlic cloves, crushed

300g (10oz) chorizo sausage, skin removed, cut into 1cm (½ in) cubes

1 tbsp tomato paste

1 tbsp fresh oregano, finely chopped

1 x 400g (14oz) can cooked lentils, rinsed and drained

3 x large tomatoes, roughly chopped

1 medium carrot, finely chopped

3 cups (750ml, 24fl oz) beef stock

1 tsp Worcestershire sauce

Salt and pepper, to taste

## METHOD

1. Heat the oil over medium heat in a large pot.

2. Fry the onion for 5 minutes until softened.

3. Add the garlic and chorizo and fry for 3 minutes until chorizo is slightly charred.

4. Stir in the tomato paste for 1 minute.

5. Add the oregano, lentils, tomatoes, carrot, stock and Worcestershire sauce and bring to a boil.

6. Reduce heat and simmer, covered, for 15 minutes.

7. Season to taste with salt and pepper and serve.

SERVES 2 ★ PREP 15MIN ★ COOK TIME 35MIN

# BEEF PHO

## INGREDIENTS

150g (5oz) noodles
(omit if following a strict
low-carb diet)

1 tsp sesame oil

3 cups (750ml, 24fl oz)
beef stock

1 tsp ginger, finely
chopped

1 garlic clove, crushed

1 star anise

2 tbsps chives, chopped

300g (10oz) sirloin
steak, sliced as thinly as
possible

2 spring onions, cut into
4cm (1½ in) lengths

1 tsp fish sauce

1 tbsp fresh lime juice

Salt and pepper

2 sprigs fresh mint,
to garnish

1 small red chilli, sliced

## METHOD

1. If using noodles, prepare these first. Boil the noodles for 3 minutes, then drain and stir through sesame oil. Place into serving bowls and set aside.

2. Simmer the stock with the ginger, garlic, star anise and half the chives for at least 30 minutes.

3. Add the beef, spring onions, fish sauce and lime juice and simmer for a further 5 minutes, until the beef is cooked.

4. Season to taste with salt and pepper.

5. Serve the hot soup poured over the noodles, and garnish with mint leaves, the rest of the chives and the chilli.

# ROAST BEEF SALAD WITH SMOKED PAPRIKA AIOLI

## INGREDIENTS

**Aioli**

1 cup (250ml, 8fl oz) olive oil

1 whole egg

1 small lemon, juiced

1 garlic clove, minced

¼ tsp smoked paprika

¼ tsp tomato paste

Salt and pepper, to taste

**Salad**

1 large beetroot

12 cherry tomatoes

2½ tsps coconut oil

Salt and pepper

300g (10oz) sirloin steak

2½ cups (75g, 3oz) mixed salad leaves

1 small red capsicum, chopped

1 small red onion, halved and thinly sliced

¼ cup (10g, ¼ oz) flat-leaf parsley, roughly chopped

1 large avocado, sliced

## METHOD

1. Preheat the oven to 180°C (350°F, Gas Mark 4) and line a baking tray with baking paper.

2. Make the aioli first by pureeing together the olive oil, egg and lemon juice until it forms a creamy mayonnaise.

3. Whisk in the garlic, paprika and tomato paste and season to taste with salt and pepper. Set aside.

4. Peel the beetroot and cut into 1½ cm (¾ in) cubes. Toss with the tomatoes in ½ tsp of coconut oil and a good couple of grinds of salt and pepper.

5. Place the beetroot on the baking tray and bake for 15 minutes. Add the tomatoes and bake for a further 15 minutes. Remove from oven and set aside.

6. Heat the rest of the coconut oil in a frying pan to medium-high heat.

7. Fry the steaks for 5 minutes each side until medium-rare or cook longer to taste. Remove from pan and let sit for 5 minutes.

8. Slice steaks into 1cm (½ in) thick slices.

9. Toss together the salad leaves, capsicum, onion, parsley, beetroot and tomatoes.

10. Layer the avocado slices on top and arrange the steak slices on top of the avocado.

11. Season with salt and pepper and top with a dollop of the paprika aioli.

# CHICKPEA MASH

## INGREDIENTS

1 tsp coconut oil

1 garlic clove, crushed

2 cups (320g, 11oz)
cooked chickpeas

1 tbsp tahini

2 tsps butter

1 tsp lime juice

## METHOD

1.  Heat the coconut oil in a medium saucepan over medium heat. Fry the garlic for 1 minute. Stir in the chickpeas and fry for 2 minutes.

2.  Reduce heat to low and mash the chickpeas with the garlic using a fork or potato masher. And add the tahini, butter, lime juice and a couple of good grinds of salt and pepper. Heat through over low heat for 10 minutes.

# PORK GOULASH

## INGREDIENTS

1 tbsp coconut oil

2 garlic cloves, crushed

1 large brown onion, chopped

700g (1½ lb) lean pork steak, cubed

1 tbsp tomato paste

1 tsp sweet paprika

1 tsp caraway seeds

1 tsp dried basil

1 large red capsicum, chopped

2 medium carrots, diced

1 x 400g (14oz) can chopped tomatoes

4 cups (1L, 2pt) beef stock

Salt and pepper

¼ cup (5g, ¼ oz) loosely packed basil leaves

## METHOD

1. Heat the oil in a large heavy-based pot.

2. Fry the garlic and onion for 5 minutes, until the onion starts to brown.

3. Add the pork and fry for a further 5 minutes to brown the pork pieces.

4. Stir in the tomato paste, paprika, caraway seeds and dried basil and fry for 1 minute.

5. Add the capsicum, carrots, tomatoes, and beef stock.

6. Bring to a boil, then reduce to barely simmering.

7. Cover and cook for 1½ hours on low heat until the pork is tender.

8. Season to taste with salt and pepper.

9. Serve garnished with fresh basil leaves.

# PORK CHOP WITH SWEET POTATO MASH

## INGREDIENTS

4 tbsps maple syrup

2 tbsps seeded mustard

1 tbsp apple cider vinegar

2 medium sweet potatoes, peeled and cut into roughly 2cm (1in) cubes

1 garlic clove, peeled

1 tsp unsalted butter

Salt and pepper

300g (10oz) green beans, ends trimmed

2 x 200g (7oz) pork chops

2 tsps paprika

2 tsps rosemary, chopped

½ cup (125ml, 4fl oz) beef stock

## METHOD

1. Whisk together the maple syrup, mustard and vinegar in a small bowl and set aside.

2. Bring a medium pot of salted water to boil and add the sweet potato and garlic.

3. Boil for 15 minutes or until the potato has softened.

4. Drain and mash the potatoes and garlic and mix together thoroughly.

5. Stir in the butter and season to taste. Keep covered and set aside.

6. Steam the green beans for 5 minutes until tender, but still firm. Remove from heat and set aside.

7. Coat the pork chops in the paprika and half the rosemary and a couple of grinds of salt and pepper, then brush with 1 tablespoon of the maple sauce.

8. Heat a frying pan over medium-high heat.

9. Grill the chops for 7 minutes per side until cooked through. Remove from pan, set aside and cover.

10. Add the rest of the maple mixture and the beef stock to the pan. Bring to the boil and then simmer for 5 minutes. Remove the sauce from the pan and pour into a small sauce jug.

11. Serve the chops over the mash and beans.

12. Drizzle over the sauce and garnish with the rest of the rosemary.

# FIG AND ROSEMARY ROASTED LAMB BACKSTRAP

## INGREDIENTS

400g (14oz) lamb backstrap fillets

6 purple figs, halved

1 tbsp olive oil

1 tbsp rosemary, finely chopped, plus 1 tbsp rosemary leaves for garnish

Salt and pepper

½ cup (125ml, 4fl oz) balsamic vinegar

1 tbsp maple syrup

## METHOD

1. Preheat the oven to 180°C (350°F, Gas Mark 4).

2. Season the lamb and figs with half the oil, chopped rosemary and 1 tsp each of salt and pepper.

3. Place the figs in a medium baking dish and bake in the oven for 10 minutes.

4. Meanwhile, heat a medium frying pan on medium-high heat.

5. Sear the lamb for 1 minute on each side then place in the baking dish with the figs after they've baked for 10 minutes and bake the lamb and figs for 15 minutes in the oven.

6. Meanwhile, heat the rest of the olive oil, balsamic vinegar, maple syrup and a dash of salt in the frying pan until nearly bubbling.

7. Reduce heat to low and cook for 5 minutes.

8. Pour over the lamb and figs before the last 5 minutes of baking.

9. Once the lamb is out of the oven, let it sit for 5 minutes before slicing.

10. Serve garnished with the rosemary leaves.

SERVES 4 ★ PREP 15MIN ★ COOK TIME 2HR, 15MIN

# FARMHOUSE STEW

## INGREDIENTS

800g (1¾ lb) stewing
beef, fat trimmed

2 tbsps olive oil

Salt and pepper,
to taste

4 medium onions,
peeled and quartered

3 garlic cloves, crushed

½ cup (125ml, 4fl oz)
red wine

2 tbsps tomato paste

1 tbsp fresh thyme,
chopped

2 tbsps red wine vinegar

300g (10oz) mushrooms,
quartered

3 medium carrots,
halved lengthways
and sliced

500g (1lb 2oz) butternut
pumpkin, cut into 3cm
(1in) chunks

2 cups (500ml, 1pt)
beef stock

2 bay leaves

## METHOD

1. Preheat the oven to 170°C (340°F, Gas Mark 4).

2. Toss the beef with half the oil and a good couple of grinds of salt
   and pepper.

3. Heat the rest of the oil in a large oven-proof casserole dish over
   medium heat. Fry the onion and garlic for 5 minutes. Add the beef
   and brown in batches, 5 minutes for each batch. Remove each
   batch from the pan and set aside.

4. Pour the red wine into the pan and bring to a boil, stirring to remove
   any bits of meat from the bottom of the pan. Simmer for 2 minutes.

5. Add the tomato paste, thyme and vinegar and fry for a further
   2 minutes. Add the mushrooms, carrot and pumpkin to the pot and
   cook for 5 minutes.

6. Return the beef to the pot and pour over the stock and add the bay
   leaves.

7. Bake in the oven for 2 hours until the beef is tender. Remove from
   oven, season to taste and serve.

# CURRIED PORK MEATBALLS

## INGREDIENTS

### Meatballs

300g (10oz) minced pork

1 small zucchini, shredded and squeezed to remove any liquid

1 tbsp coriander, finely chopped

1 tsp cumin

½ small onion, pureed

1 garlic clove, crushed

1 tbsp coconut oil

### Sauce

1 tbsp green curry paste

1 tbsp coriander, finely chopped

¾ cup (185ml, 6fl oz) vegetable stock

½ cup (125ml, 4fl oz) coconut milk

2 tsps fish sauce

2 tsps lime juice

¼ cup (5g, ¼ oz) loosely packed Thai basil leaves

Salt and pepper, to taste

## METHOD

1.  In a large bowl, mix together the meatball ingredients, except for the coconut oil. Form the meat into 12 meatballs.

2.  Melt the coconut oil in a medium, deep-sided frying pan over medium-high heat. Fry the meatballs for about 2 minutes each on four sides. Remove from the pan.

3.  Stir the curry paste into the pan for 1 minute.

4.  Add the coriander, stock, coconut milk, fish sauce, lime juice and half of the basil leaves.

5.  Add the meatballs. Bring to a simmer.

6.  Cover and let cook for 15 minutes.

7.  Season to taste.

8.  Serve garnished with remaining basil leaves.

# PERFECT ROAST BEEF

## INGREDIENTS

2 garlic cloves, crushed

2 tbsps thyme leaves, finely chopped

2 tsps rosemary, finely chopped

1 tbsp Dijon mustard

1 tsp soy sauce

1 tsp ground cumin

1 tbsp coconut oil

Salt and pepper, to taste

1kg (2lb) sirloin top roast

3 sprigs thyme, to garnish

## METHOD

1. Mix together the garlic, chopped thyme, rosemary, Dijon, soy, cumin, coconut oil and a couple of good grinds of salt and pepper.

2. Coat the meat in the paste and then sit, covered, in the refrigerator for 1 hour.

3. To slow roast so that the meat is tender and falls apart:

   Preheat the oven to 150°C (300°F, Gas Mark 2).

   Place the meat in the oven, uncovered, along with a small oven-proof bowl filled with water.

   Roast for 4 hours, ensuring that there is always at least 2cm (1in) of water in the bowl to keep the roast moist.

   The roast will then be cooked through, but tender and break apart easily.

4. To roast rare to well-done:

   Preheat the oven to 180°C (350°F, Gas Mark 4).

   To cook rare: Roast for 40 minutes (20 minutes per 450g).

   To cook to medium: roast for 50 minutes (25 minutes per 450g).

   To cook to well-done: roast for 1 hour (30 minutes per 450g).

5. Once cooked to taste, remove from oven and let sit for 5 minutes, covered, before slicing to serve.

# SLOW-COOKED LAMB STEW

## INGREDIENTS

1 tbsp coconut oil

2 medium onions, chopped

3 garlic cloves, crushed

1kg (2lb) lamb fillet, cut into 3cm (1in) chunks

1 tbsp tomato paste

2 tsps oregano, finely chopped

1 large red capsicum, chopped

3 large tomatoes, chopped

1 small red chilli, minced

½ cup (125ml, 4fl oz) red wine

2 cups (500ml, 1pt) vegetable stock

½ cup (70g, 2½ oz) black olives, pitted and halved

Salt and pepper

## METHOD

1.  Preheat the oven to 160°C (325°F, Gas Mark 3).

2.  Heat the oil in a large oven-proof casserole dish over medium heat. Fry the onion for 5 minutes until softened. Add the garlic and fry for 1 minute.

3.  Fry the lamb in batches for 5 minutes each time or until browned. Transfer lamb to a bowl and set aside.

4.  Add the tomato paste and oregano and stir for 1 minute. Add the capsicum, tomatoes and chilli and cook for 2 minutes. Pour in the red wine and bring to a boil for 2 minutes. Add the stock and bring to a boil again.

5.  Place the lid on the dish and put in the oven. Cook for 2 hours or until lamb is starting to become tender.

6.  Remove from the oven and stir in the olives. Return to the oven and cook for 30 minutes.

7.  Remove from the oven and season to taste with salt and pepper. Serve warm.

# BEEF MADRAS

## INGREDIENTS

2 tbsps coconut oil

1kg (2lb) stewing steak, cut into 2cm (1in) cubes

2 tbsps ground coriander

1 tbsp garam masala

½ tsp fresh ginger, grated

1 tsp lemon juice

2 tbsps tomato paste

2 large tomatoes, chopped

1 cup (250ml, 8fl oz) beef stock

4 tbsps natural yoghurt

Salt and pepper

1 tbsps fresh coriander, finely chopped

## METHOD

1.  Heat the oil in a large, deep-sided saucepan over high heat. Fry the beef in batches for 5 minutes each time or until browned. Transfer beef to a bowl and set aside.

2.  Reduce heat to medium. Fry the coriander, garam masala, ginger, lemon juice and tomato paste for 2 minutes until fragrant.

3.  Return the beef to the pan and stir to coat in the paste. Add the tomato and stock and bring to the boil.

4.  Reduce heat and gently simmer, covered, for 1½ hours.

5.  Stir the yoghurt into the pan.

6.  Season to taste with salt and pepper and serve garnished with fresh coriander.

# ROASTED LAMB CHOPS WITH KALE

## INGREDIENTS

2 tbsps coconut oil

2 garlic cloves, crushed

¼ tsp turmeric

½ tsp cumin

½ tsp ground oregano

Salt and pepper

½ bunch kale, chopped

1 x 400g (14oz) can cannellini beans, rinsed and drained

Pinch of nutmeg

½ tbsp lemon juice

¼ cup (60ml, 2fl oz) vegetable stock

400g (14oz) lamb chops

2 sprigs flat-leaf parsley, to garnish

## METHOD

1. Preheat the oven to 200°C (400°F, Gas Mark 6) and line a baking tray with baking paper.

2. In a small bowl, mix together half the coconut oil, half the garlic, the turmeric, cumin, oregano, ½ teaspoon salt and a good grind of pepper. Rub into the lamb chops and set aside.

3. In a medium-sized saucepan, heat the rest of the oil over medium heat.

4. Fry the rest of the garlic for one minute, then add the kale in batches. Once the kale is softened, stir through the beans, nutmeg, lemon juice and stock. Lower the heat, cover and cook for 10 minutes while you prepare the lamb.

5. Heat a large frying pan to medium-high heat.

6. Fry the lamb chops for 2 minutes on each side to sear in the juices.

7. Place the lamb on the baking tray and bake for 5 minutes until slightly browned.

8. Season the kale to taste with more salt and pepper.

9. Serve the lamb on top of the kale and beans, garnished with parsley.

# CHILLI CON CARNE

## INGREDIENTS

2 tbsps olive oil

2 medium onions, chopped

3 garlic cloves, crushed

1 tbsp ground oregano

2 tsps cayenne pepper

1 tsp ground chilli

2 tsps cumin

¼ tsp ground cinnamon

500g (1lb 2oz) lean minced beef

½ cup (125ml, 4fl oz) dry red wine

1 cup (250ml, 8fl oz) beef stock

1 cup (170g, 6oz) corn kernels

1 x 400g (14oz) can chopped tomatoes

1 x 400g (14oz) can kidney beans, rinsed and drained

1 tbsp flat-leaf parsley, roughly chopped

Salt and pepper

4 sprigs flat-leaf parsley, to garnish

1 spring onion, sliced, to garnish

## METHOD

1.  In a large frying pan, heat the oil over medium-high heat.

2.  Fry the onion for 5 minutes until softened and browned.

3.  Add the garlic and herbs and spices and fry for a further minute.

4.  Add the mince and fry for 7 minutes until browned.

5.  Pour in the wine and bring to a boil.

6.  Add the rest of the ingredients, bring to a boil, then reduce heat to a simmer.

7.  Cover and simmer for 1 hour.

8.  Season to taste with salt and pepper and serve garnished with the parsley and spring onion.

# PORK LARB

**INGREDIENTS**

3 tbsps coconut oil

1 red onion, halved and sliced

2 spring onions, sliced

1 stem lemongrass, pale section only, finely chopped

1 small chilli, finely chopped

2 garlic cloves, crushed

2 tbsps fresh ginger, finely chopped

½ bunch coriander leaves, finely chopped

500g (1lb 2oz) pork fillet, cut into small thin 2cm (1in) strips

¼ cup (60ml, 2fl oz) lime juice

2 tbsps fish sauce

1 tsp sesame oil

1 tbsp palm sugar

2 tbsps tamari sauce

1 cup (15g, ½ oz) loosely packed mint leaves

Salt and pepper

**METHOD**

1. Heat the coconut oil in a large deep-sided frying pan or wok over high heat.

2. Quickly stir in the onion, spring onions, lemongrass, chilli, garlic, ginger and coriander and fry for 1 minute.

3. And the pork and a quarter of the lime juice. Stir fry the pork for 8 minutes until cooked through.

4. Stir in the rest of the lime juice, the fish sauce, sesame oil, sugar and tamari sauce and heat through for 2 minutes.

5. Remove from heat and stir in half the mint leaves.

6. Season to taste with salt and pepper and serve garnished with the rest of the mint leaves.

# THAI BEEF SALAD

## INGREDIENTS

300g (10oz) sirloin steak

1 tsp peanut oil

½ iceberg lettuce, shredded

8 cherry tomatoes, halved

1 medium Lebanese cucumber, cut into matchsticks

½ cup (20g, ¾ oz) mint leaves, plus extra to garnish

¼ cup (20g, ¾ oz) coriander leaves, roughly chopped

1 red chilli, thinly sliced

¼ cup (30g, 1oz) peanuts, roughly chopped

½ cup (50g, 2oz) bean sprouts, rinsed

### Dressing

1½ tbsps fresh lime juice

1½ tbsps peanut oil

½ tbsp soy sauce

½ tbsp fish sauce

½ tsp sesame oil

½ tbsps brown sugar

1 small garlic clove, crushed

1 tbsp fresh ginger, minced

## METHOD

1. Mix together the dressing ingredients with half the peanuts in a small bowl and set aside.

2. Heat a grill pan to high heat. Lightly oil the steak with peanut oil. Grill on each side for 4 minutes to cook to medium rare. For well done meat, leave on the grill for a further 3 minutes or until cooked through. Remove from the pan and let sit for 5 minutes.

3. To make the salad, toss together the lettuce, tomatoes, cucumber, mint, coriander, half the chilli and the rest of the peanuts.

4. Slice the steak as thinly as you can, and layer on top of the salad.

5. Pour the dressing over the top.

6. Garnish with extra mint leaves, bean sprouts and the rest of the chilli.

# STICKY PORK RIBS

## INGREDIENTS

1 cup (250ml, 8fl oz) soy sauce

1 cup (250ml, 8fl oz) sake (optional)

1 tsp cayenne pepper

4 tbsps maple syrup

1 tbsp fresh ginger, minced

2 garlic cloves, crushed

6 tbsps sesame oil

2 sides (1¼ kg/3lb 4oz) pork ribs

## METHOD

1. Combine all ingredients except the ribs in a jar with a secure-fitting lid. Shake to combine.

2. Place the ribs in a container large enough to stack them one on top of the other.

3. Pour the marinade over the ribs and turn to coat, rubbing the marinade in with your fingers.

4. Cover with plastic wrap and transfer to the refrigerator to marinate overnight.

5. Preheat the oven to 150°C (300°F, gas mark 2).

6. Remove ribs from the refrigerator and set aside half of the marinade.

7. Place the ribs with the other half of the marinade in a baking tray. Transfer to the oven and bake, turning the ribs frequently, for 2 hours, or until the meat is tender.

8. Heat a grill pan over medium-high heat. Finish the ribs by cooking each side for 3-4 minutes.

9. Remove the ribs and cut each side into individual pieces.

10. Heat the reserved marinade in a small saucepan until bubbling. Reduce to a simmer and cook for 4 minutes.

11. Serve sauce on the side.

SERVES 4 ★ PREP 10MIN ★ COOK TIME 8MIN

# LAMB CUTLETS WITH MINT SAUCE

## INGREDIENTS

400g (14oz) Frenched lamb cutlets

1 tsp coconut oil

Salt and pepper

Mint leaves, to garnish

**Sauce**

1 garlic clove, crushed

¼ cup (10g, ¼ oz) flat-leaf parsley, finely chopped

¼ cup (10g, ¼ oz) fresh mint leaves, finely chopped

2 tbsps lemon juice

½ tbsp olive oil

1 tsp apple cider vinegar

Salt and pepper, to taste

## METHOD

1. Mix together all the ingredients for the sauce in a small bowl. Set aside.

2. Rub the lamb with the coconut oil and a couple of good grinds of salt and pepper.

3. Heat a grill pan over high heat.

4. Fry the lamb cutlets for 4 minutes on each side or until cooked to your liking.

5. Let the cutlets sit, covered, for a couple of minutes.

6. Serve with the sauce drizzled over the top of the cutlets and garnished with mint leaves.

# LAMB SHANKS IN RED WINE SAUCE

## INGREDIENTS

1 tbsp coconut oil

2 lamb shanks

1 medium onion, chopped

2 garlic cloves, crushed

1 small carrot, finely chopped

½ cup (125ml, 4fl oz) dry red wine

1 cup (250ml, 8fl oz) beef stock

¼ cup (10g, ¼ oz) flat-leaf parsley, roughly chopped

Salt and pepper

2 sprigs flat-leaf parsley, to garnish

## METHOD

1. Preheat the oven to 190°C (375°F, Gas Mark 5).

2. In a medium-sized oven-proof casserole dish, heat the oil over medium-high heat. Fry the shanks for 2 minutes to lightly brown them. Remove from the dish and set aside.

3. Fry the onion for 5 minutes until softened and browned. Add the garlic and carrot and fry for 1 further minute. Pour in the wine and bring to a boil.

4. Return the shanks to the dish and pour the stock over the top. Stir in the parsley. Cover and bake in the oven for 1 hour and 20 minutes. Check the level of liquid during this time and top up if needed.

5. Once cooked, remove from the oven and let the shanks sit for 5 minutes. Season to taste with salt and pepper and serve garnished with parsley.

# BURGER 'N' SALAD

## INGREDIENTS

500g (1lb 2oz) minced
lean lamb

1 tbsp fresh mint,
finely chopped

1 tsp dried oregano

2 spring onions,
finely chopped

Salt and pepper

4 rashers bacon

1½ tbsps coconut oil

450g (1lb) green beans

¼ cup (30g, 1oz)
almonds, chopped

2 large tomatoes,
sliced

8 butter lettuce leaves

1 large avocado,
halved and sliced

1 large red onion,
sliced into rings

## METHOD

1.  In a large bowl, combine the lamb, mint, oregano, spring onion and
    a couple of good grinds of salt and pepper.

2.  Shape the mixture into four patties.

3.  Heat a large frying pan over medium-high heat and fry the bacon
    for 8 minutes until crispy. Remove from pan and set aside

4.  Heat half the oil in the pan. Place the burgers on the pan and flatten
    slightly with a spatula. Cook the burgers 5 minutes on each side,
    taking care to turn them over so they stay together. Set aside.

5.  Heat the rest of the oil in the pan and fry the beans for 5 minutes
    until tender and slightly charred. Add the almonds and fry 1 further
    minute.

6.  Serve by layering equal portions of tomatoes and bacon on top of
    2 lettuce leaves for each serving plate. Place a burger on top and
    then garnish with the avocado and onion. Serve the beans and
    almonds on the side.

# VEGETABLES AND SIDES

# HOMEMADE TOMATO SOUP

## INGREDIENTS

2 tbsps coconut oil

1 medium onion, chopped

3 garlic cloves, crushed

1 tbsp tomato paste

½ red capsicum, chopped

2 x 400g (14oz) cans diced tomatoes

2 cups (500ml, 1pt) vegetable stock

1 cup (250ml, 8fl oz) coconut milk

1 tbsp finely chopped rosemary plus 1 sprig rosemary leaves, to garnish

Salt and pepper

## METHOD

1. Heat the oil in a large pot over medium heat.

2. Fry the onion for 5 minutes until softened and browned.

3. Add the garlic and fry for 1 further minute.

4. Mix in the tomato paste and capsicum and cook for another 1 minute.

5. Add the tomatoes, stock, coconut milk and chopped rosemary and bring to the boil.

6. Reduce the heat to low and simmer, covered, for 30 minutes.

7. Remove from heat and let cool for 10 minutes.

8. Use a blender stick to puree the soup until smooth.

9. Season to taste with salt and pepper and serve garnished with rosemary leaves.

# ROCKET AND FIG SALAD WITH BALSAMIC GLAZE

### INGREDIENTS

¾ cup (90g, 3oz) pecans

3 cups (90g, 3oz) rocket
leaves, washed and dried

2 large green figs,
cut into quarters

¾ cup (180g, 6oz) feta

### Glaze

1 cup (250ml, 8fl oz)
balsamic vinegar

2 tbsps brown sugar

Pinch of salt

### METHOD

1.  Dry fry the pecans in a small frying pan over medium heat for 2 minutes until just starting to brown. Remove immediately from the pan and set aside.

2.  To make the glaze, heat the vinegar in a medium frying pan over medium heat until simmering. Cook for 10 minutes until reduced by about half. Add the sugar and salt and stir until dissolved. Remove from heat into a pouring jug.

3.  Arrange the rocket, figs, feta and pecans on your serving plates.

4.  Drizzle over the glaze and serve.

# CHEESE AND TOMATO PIZZA ON CAULIFLOWER CRUST

## INGREDIENTS

1 x cooked cauliflower crust (see recipe on page 112)

2 tbsps tomato paste

2 tsps water

1 tsp dried mixed herbs

½ tsp olive oil

1 small garlic clove, crushed

¾ cup (90g, 3oz) mozzarella, grated

2 large tomatoes, sliced

½ cup (20g, ¾ oz) fresh basil, roughly chopped

## METHOD

1. Preheat the oven to 230°C (445°F, Gas Mark 8).

2. In a small bowl, mix together the tomato paste, water, mixed herbs, olive oil and garlic.

3. Spread the tomato sauce evenly over the pizza crust.

4. Sprinkle the mozzarella evenly over the sauce.

5. Arrange the tomato slices over the pizza.

6. Bake for 10 minutes, then remove from the oven and top with the basil.

7. Return to the oven and bake for a further 2 minutes.

8. Serve warm.

SERVES 4 ★ PREP 15MIN ★ COOK TIME 15MIN

# RAW KALE AND DILL SALAD

**INGREDIENTS**

**Dressing**

⅓ cup (80ml, 3fl oz) olive oil

⅓ cup (80ml, 3fl oz) red wine vinegar

1 tbsp brown sugar

1 tsp lemon juice

1 small garlic clove, crushed

¼ cup (10g, ¼ oz) fresh dill, roughly chopped (retain a few sprigs to garnish)

Salt and pepper, to taste

**Salad**

1¼ cups (210g, 8oz) white quinoa

2 cups (500ml, 1pt) vegetable stock

¾ cup (90g, 3oz) slivered almonds

1 bunch curly kale, washed and dried, cut into 2cm (1in) pieces

100g (3½ oz) feta cheese

½ cup (80g, 3oz) dried prunes

**METHOD**

1. To make the dressing, combine all the dressing ingredients in small bowl. Set aside.
2. Rinse quinoa in cold water. Add to a medium-sized pot with cold stock. Bring to a boil. Reduce heat and simmer, covered, for 15 minutes. Drain and set aside.
3. Toss together the kale, quinoa, almonds, feta and prunes.
4. Drizzle over the dressing, garnish with retained dill sprigs and serve.

# BEETROOT BORSCHT

## INGREDIENTS

1 tbsp coconut oil

1 large onion, finely chopped

2 garlic cloves, crushed

3 large beetroots, peeled, 1 x grated, 2 x cut into 1½ cm (¾ in) cubes

1 medium potato cut into 1½ cm (¾ in) cubes

2 large carrots, cut into 1½ cm (¾ in) cubes

4 cups (1L, 2pt) vegetable stock

1 tsp tamari sauce

2 tbsps apple cider vinegar

1 tbsp lemon juice

¼ cup (35g, 1¼ oz) pickled gherkins, diced

¼ cup (10g, ¼ oz) fresh dill, roughly chopped

Salt and pepper

## METHOD

1. Heat the oil in a large pot over medium-high heat.

2. Fry the onion for 5 minutes until softened and browned.

3. Add the garlic and fry for 1 further minute. Add the beetroot, potato and carrots and cook for 5 minutes.

4. Add the stock, tamari, vinegar and lemon juice and bring to a boil.

5. Reduce the heat and simmer, covered, for 40 minutes, until the vegetables are tender.

6. Stir in the gherkins and half the dill and simmer for a further 5 minutes.

7. Season to taste with salt and pepper and serve garnished with the rest of the dill.

SERVES 2 ★ PREP 20MIN

# EGGPLANT CAPRESE

## INGREDIENTS

4 tbsps olive oil

2 medium eggplants,
sliced into 1cm (½ in)
rounds

1 large ball mozzarella,
sliced into 1cm (½ in)
rounds

2 large tomatoes,
sliced into 1cm (½ in)
rounds

2 tbsps olive oil

2 tbsps balsamic vinegar

2 tbsps pesto (see recipe
on page 78)

Pepper, to taste

¼ cup (10g, ¼ oz)
fresh basil leaves

## METHOD

1. Brush the eggplant slices with half the olive oil and a good couple of grinds of salt and pepper.

2. Heat a large grill pan over medium-high heat.

3. Grill the eggplant slices for 5 minutes on either side until softened.

4. Arrange the eggplant slices on a serving place in overlapping circles with the mozzarella and tomato slices.

5. Drizzle over the oil, vinegar and pesto.

6. Garnish with basil leaves.

# GREEN PEA SALAD WITH MISO DRESSING

## INGREDIENTS

### Dressing

3 tbsps lemon juice

2 tbsps dark miso paste

1 tsp fresh ginger, minced

2 tbsps soy sauce

4 tbsps honey

3 tbsps toasted sesame oil

### Salad

1 head of broccoli, broken into florets

2 cups (300g, 10oz) sugar snap peas, trimmed

1 cup (150g, 5oz) shelled peas (fresh or frozen)

2 heads baby cos lettuce, leaves pulled apart

1 avocado, sliced

1 Lebanese cucumber, sliced

2 tbsps black sesame seeds

## METHOD

1. To make the dressing, whisk together the dressing ingredients in a bowl and set aside.

2. Steam the broccoli for 5 minutes or until firm but tender. Rinse in cold water then place in a large mixing bowl.

3. Steam the sugar snap peas and shelled peas for 3 minutes, until firm but tender. Rinse under cold water and also place in the bowl with the broccoli.

4. Toss together the lettuce, avocado and cucumber with the cooked vegetables.

5. Drizzle over the miso dressing and sprinkle the black sesame seeds on top.

# QUICK PICKLED CUCUMBER

## INGREDIENTS

1 cup (250ml, 8fl oz) rice wine vinegar

2½ tbsps light brown sugar

¾ tsp salt

3 tsps sesame oil

1 tbsp fresh dill, finely chopped

½ tbsp fresh oregano, finely chopped

1 tsp pepper

3 medium Lebanese cucumbers, cut into 3mm (⅛ in) thick slices

## METHOD

1. Heat the vinegar, sugar and salt in a small saucepan over low heat for 10 minutes or until the sugar is dissolved.

2. Remove from heat and whisk in the oil, dill, oregano and pepper.

3. Layer the cucumbers in a container that has a sealable lid.

4. Pour over the vinegar mixture.

5. Seal the container and place in the refrigerator for a least 4 hours, preferably overnight.

6. Will keep for about 3-4 days in the refrigerator.

# TOFU-VEG STIR FRY

### INGREDIENTS

**Sauce**

3 tbsps tamari sauce

1 tbsp lime juice

1 tsp fish sauce

1 tbsp fresh ginger, finely chopped

2 tbsps light brown sugar

1 tbsp agave syrup

**Stir fry**

400g (14oz) firm tofu, cut into 3cm (1in) cubes

1 tsp tumeric

1 sheet of nori seaweed, cut into very small pieces

Salt and pepper

1 tbsp coconut oil

2 cups (230g, 8oz) sugar snap peas, ends trimmed

1 long red chilli, seeded and sliced

### METHOD

1.  Whisk together all the sauce ingredients in a small bowl and set aside.

2.  Pat dry the tofu. Toss with tumeric, nori and a couple of good grinds of salt and pepper.

3.  Heat the coconut oil in a wok over high heat. Fry the tofu for 4 minutes until it starts to brown. Add the sugar snap peas and chilli and stir fry for 1 further minute.

4.  Give the sauce a quick whisk and then add to the wok. Stir to coat the tofu and vegetables for another 1 minute and remove from the heat.

# MOROCCAN SPICED SOUP

## INGREDIENTS

¼ cup (30g, 1oz) pistachios, chopped

2 tbsps coconut oil

1 large onion, chopped

2 garlic cloves, minced

1 tsp fresh ginger, minced

2 tsps cumin

2 tsps ground oregano

½ tsp turmeric

2 medium carrots, chopped

1 medium cauliflower, broken into florets

1 large red apple, chopped

¼ cup (10g, ¼ oz) fresh coriander, roughly chopped

2 cups (500ml, 1pt) vegetable stock

½ cup (125ml, 4fl oz) coconut milk

1 tsp tamari sauce

Salt and pepper

## METHOD

1. Heat a small frying pan over medium heat and dry fry the pistachios for 3 minutes. Remove from heat and set aside.

2. Heat the coconut oil in a large pot over medium-high heat.

3. Fry the onion for 5 minutes until softened and browned.

4. Add the garlic and ginger and fry for a further 1 minute. Add the cumin, oregano and turmeric and fry for another 1 minute.

5. Add the carrots, cauliflower and apple and cook for 5 minutes.

6. Add half the coriander, the stock, coconut milk, tamari and half the pistachios. Bring to a boil then reduce to a simmer. Cover and simmer gently for 30 minutes until the vegetables have softened.

7. Let cool for 10 minutes.

8. Use a stick blender to puree the soup until smooth.

9. Season to taste with salt and pepper and serve garnished with the remaining pistachios and coriander leaves.

**SERVES 4 ★ PREP 25MIN**

# CRUNCHY CABBAGE SALAD

## INGREDIENTS

¼ cup (30g, 1oz) pumpkin seeds (pepitas)

1 tbsp fresh dill, finely chopped

½ large head of white cabbage, shredded

2 cups (200g, 7oz) celery, sliced

3 cups (150g, 5oz) curly endive leaves, roughly chopped

¼ cup (60ml, 2fl oz) olive oil

1 tbsp apple cider vinegar

Salt and pepper

## METHOD

1. Dry fry the pumpkin seeds in a small frying pan over medium-high heat for 2 minutes until just starting to brown. Remove immediately from the pan.

2. Toss the pumpkin seeds, dill, cabbage, celery and endive together in a large bowl.

3. Whisk together the oil and vinegar with a couple of good grinds of salt and pepper and toss with the salad.

4. Season to taste and serve.

# EGGPLANT RATATOUILLE

## INGREDIENTS

2 tbsps olive oil

1 small onion, finely chopped

2 garlic cloves, crushed

1 cup (225g, 8oz) tomato passata

3 large eggplants, halved and cut into 3mm thick slices

2 medium zucchini, cut into 3mm (⅛ in) rounds

2 small yellow squash, cut into 3mm (⅛ in) slices

1 tsp chilli flakes

1 tbsp fresh oregano, finely chopped

2 tbsps herbs de Provence

Salt and pepper

1 x 210g (7fl oz) can crushed tomatoes

¼ cup (10g, ¼ oz) basil leaves, roughly chopped

2 tbsps Parmesan, grated

Sprig basil leaves, to garnish

## METHOD

1. Preheat the oven to 180°C (350°F, Gas Mark 4) and lightly oil a 30cm x 20cm baking dish.

2. Heat half the olive oil in a small frying pan.

3. Fry the onion for 5 minutes until softened and browned.

4. Add the garlic and fry for 1 further minute.

5. Pour in ½ cup of the tomato puree and cook for 3 minutes. Remove from heat.

6. Toss the eggplant, zucchini and squash with the rest of the olive oil, the chilli, herbs and a couple of good grinds of salt and pepper.

7. Place the sliced vegetables in rows, edges down, in the dish. Alternate a slice of eggplant, then zucchini, then squash.

8. Mix the rest of the sauce with the crushed tomatoes, remaining tom and chopped basil and pour over the vegetables.

9. Bake for 50 minutes, until the vegetables are cooked through.

10. Sprinkle over the Parmesan and garnish with fresh basil leaves.

# SWEET POTATO BURGER

## INGREDIENTS

500g (1lb 2oz) sweet potatoes, peeled and cut into 3cm (1in) cubes

½ cup (80g, 3oz) cooked chickpeas

3 spring onions, chopped

1 egg

½ tsp turmeric

¼ cup (30g, 1oz) pistachios, finely chopped

1 small carrot, peeled and grated

Salt and pepper

2 tbsps coconut oil

½ cup (125g, 4oz) paprika aioli (recipe page 122)

## METHOD

1. Place the sweet potatoes in a large saucepan and cover with cold water. Bring to a boil then lower the heat. Cover and simmer for 8 minutes until the potatoes are tender.

2. Place the potato in a large mixing bowl with the chickpeas and use a masher to roughly mash them together.

3. Add the onions, egg, turmeric, pistachios, carrot and a couple of good grinds of salt and pepper. Mix thoroughly and form into 4 burger patties.

4. Cover the patties and place in the refrigerator to chill for at least 3 hours.

5. Heat the coconut oil in a large frying pan over high heat. Add the burgers and fry for 5 minutes on each side.

6. Serve with salad leaves and a dollop of paprika aioli.

# TZATZIKI

## INGREDIENTS

½ Continental cucumber, plus a few slices for garnish

1 small pickled gherkin

2 cloves of garlic, minced

1 cup (250ml, 8fl oz) Greek yogurt

1 tsp fresh dill, finely chopped, plus a sprig to garnish

1 tsp fresh mint, finely chopped

½ tsp lemon juice

¼ tsp olive oil

¼ tsp white wine vinegar

## METHOD

1. Peel and seed the cucumber, then grate it and squeeze out as much liquid as you can. Pat dry with paper towels.

2. Grate the gherkin and again squeeze out as much liquid as you can and pat dry with paper towels.

3. In a medium bowl, combine the cucumber and gherkin with the rest of the ingredients.

4. Serve with a sprig of dill and a few cucumber slices as garnish.

**SERVES 4  ★  PREP 15MIN  ★  COOK TIME 30MIN**

# BABA GANOUSH

## INGREDIENTS

2 medium eggplants, halved lengthways

1 sprig rosemary

2 tbsps olive oil

2 garlic cloves, crushed

1 tsp salt

2 tbsps lemon juice

3 tbsps tahini

Pepper, to taste

2 sprigs flat-leaf parsley, chopped

½ tsp smoky paprika

Sumac (or more paprika)

## METHOD

1. Preheat the oven to 200°C (400°F, Gas Mark 6) and line a baking tray with baking paper.

2. Place the eggplants on the baking tray cut side down with a sprig of rosemary and drizzle with half the olive and bake for 30 minutes or until softened.

3. Scoop out the flesh and put in a medium bowl with the baked rosemary leaves

4. Add the garlic, salt, lemon juice, tahini, a couple of good grinds of pepper, half the parsley and the paprika.

5. Blend the mixture with a stick blender until nearly smooth.

6. Season to taste.

7. Serve with the remaining parsley, a sprinkle of sumac or paprika and the rest of the olive oil drizzled on top.

# BEETROOT BEANBURGERS

## INGREDIENTS

500g (1lb 2oz) beetroots

1 cup (165g, 6oz) cooked wild rice

2 x 400g (14oz) cans kidney beans, rinsed and drained

¼ cup (45g, 1½oz) dates, pitted and chopped into small pieces

1 tbsp olive oil

1 medium onion, finely chopped

3 garlic cloves, crushed

2 tbsps apple cider vinegar

¼ cup (20g, ¾ oz) rolled oats, processed in a blender to a rough flour

1 tsp sumac

2 tsps Dijon mustard

1 tsp cumin

½ tsp ground oregano

2 tsps rosemary leaves, finely chopped

1 large egg

Salt and pepper

2 tbsps coconut oil

## METHOD

1. Preheat the oven to 200°C (400°F, Gas Mark 6).

2. Wrap the beetroots in aluminium foil and bake in the oven for 50 minutes or until tender. Remove from oven and let cool.

3. Meanwhile, add half the kidney beans to the processor and add the dates. Pulse about 10 times until the beans are chopped but not a paste. Remove to a large mixing bowl and add the rest of the beans to the bowl.

4. In a medium frying pan, heat the olive oil over medium-high heat. Fry the onion for 7 minutes until softened and browned. Add the garlic and fry for 1 minute.

5. Pour in the cider vinegar and scrape the bottom of the pan to remove any pieces stuck to it. Once the vinegar has cooked off, add the onion and garlic to the mixing bowl.

6. Once the beetroots are cooled, peel off the skin and grate them. Strain and squeeze to remove as much liquid as you can. Transfer the beetroot to the mixing bowl. Add the rest of the ingredients, except the coconut oil, including a couple of good grinds of salt and pepper and mix as thoroughly as you can. Form into 6 patties then place them, covered, in the refrigerator to chill for at least 3 hours.

7. Heat 1 tablespoon coconut oil in a large frying pan over high heat. Cook the burgers for 4 minutes on each side, taking care when flipping so they don't break apart. Add more oil as needed when cooking the burgers.

8. Serve burgers with a side of fresh salad leaves.

# CHIMICHURRI SAUCE

## INGREDIENTS

½ cup (10g, ¼ oz) fresh basil leaves, loosely packed

½ cup (10g, ¼ oz) fresh coriander leaves, loosely packed

¾ cup (185ml, 6fl oz) olive oil

3 tbsps lemon juice

2 tbsps red wine vinegar

3 garlic cloves, crushed

1 tsp capers

½ tsp dried oregano

½ tsp dried basil

½ tsp chilli flakes

Salt and pepper

## METHOD

1. Place all the ingredients together in a bowl including a couple of good grinds of salt and pepper.

2. Use a stick blender to puree the ingredients together until you have a thick sauce. Don't overblend it, you still want small bits of leaves in it.

3. Season to taste and serve.

# LOW-CARB BBQ SAUCE

## METHOD

1. Place all ingredients in a small saucepan and heat over medium-high. Include a couple of good grinds of pepper.

2. Bring to a boil, then reduce heat to low and simmer, covered, for 50 minutes.

3. Let cool for 10 minutes, then puree with a stick blender.

4. Season to taste.

## INGREDIENTS

1⅔ cups (400ml, 13fl oz) tomato sauce

2 tbsps tomato paste

1 cup (250ml, 8fl oz) water

½ small onion, finely chopped

1 garlic clove, minced

½ cup (125ml, 4fl oz) apple cider vinegar

4 tbsps maple syrup

1 tbsp lemon juice

½ tbsp Dijon mustard

1 tsp smoked paprika

½ tsp Worcestershire sauce

Salt and pepper

# VEGAN TOFU SALAD

## INGREDIENTS

300g (10oz) firm tofu, cut into 3cm (1in) cubes

1 tbsp coconut oil

½ cup (60g, 2oz) peanuts

½ cup (80g, 3oz) cooked wild rice

2 cups (230g, 8oz) sugar snap peas, ends trimmed

½ small Lebanese cucumber, peeled and cut into small chunks

1 mango, cut into cubes

½ small red onion, finely chopped

2 tbsps coriander, chopped

1 spring onion, finely chopped

Salt and pepper

**Dressing**

2 garlic cloves, crushed

1 tbsp fresh ginger, minced

2 tbsps lemongrass, finely chopped

2 tbsps tamari sauce

2 tbsps fish sauce

2 tbsps lime juice

2 tbsps agave syrup

1 tsp lemon juice

1 tsp chilli sauce

## METHOD

1. Whisk all the dressing ingredients together in a small bowl and set aside.

2. Pour 1 tablespoon of the dressing over the tofu and toss to coat.

3. Heat the oil in a wok over high heat. Add the tofu and stir fry for 4 minutes or until it starts to brown.

4. Add the peanuts and fry for another minute, stirring the whole time.

5. In a large bowl, toss together the tofu, peanuts and the rest of the salad ingredients.

6. Pour the dressing over the salad and toss again to mix thoroughly.

7. Season to taste with salt and pepper serve.

# ROASTED CAULIFLOWER SALAD

## INGREDIENTS

1 large head of cauliflower, cut into small florets

4 tbsps olive oil

1 tsp turmeric

2 tbsps dried oregano

3 tbsps balsamic vinegar

Salt and pepper, to taste

**Salad**

¾ cup (90g, 3oz) chopped walnuts

¼ cup (10g, ¼ oz) flat-leaf parsley, finely chopped

3 cups (120g, 4oz) baby spinach

1 medium red onion, finely chopped

¼ cup (50ml, 2fl oz) olive oil

## METHOD

1. Preheat the oven to 220°C (425°C, Gas Mark 7) and line a baking tray with baking paper.

2. Toss the cauliflower with the oil, turmeric and oregano. Spread the florets out evenly on the baking sheet and season with salt and pepper.

3. Roast for 8 minutes, then remove the tray and turn the pieces over. Return to the oven for another 8 minutes.

4. Sprinkle the vinegar over the cauliflower and bake for 7 minutes. Remove from the oven and let it cool.

5. Dry fry the walnuts in a small frying pan over medium heat for 2 minutes until just starting to brown. Remove immediately from the pan and set aside.

6. Toss together the cauliflower with the rest of the salad ingredients, including the olive oil.

7. Season to taste with salt and pepper and serve.

# KALE PESTO

## INGREDIENTS

¾ cup (30g, 1oz) flat-leaf parsley, roughly chopped

1½ cups (45g, 1½ oz) packed baby kale, roughly chopped

⅓ cup (80ml, 3fl oz) lemon juice

1 cup (250ml, 8fl oz) olive oil

2 small garlic cloves, crushed

½ cup (60g, 2oz) almond slivers

¼ cup (35g, 1¼ oz) pine nuts

Salt and pepper, to taste.

## METHOD

1. Place the parsley, kale, lemon juice, half the olive oil and garlic together in a mixing bowl.

2. Use a stick blender to puree the mixture to a rough sauce consistency.

3. Add the almonds and pine nuts and blend, adding the rest of the oil in small amounts until you have a thick pesto sauce.

4. Season to taste.

# LOW-CARB RANCH DRESSING

## INGREDIENTS

½ cup (125ml, 4fl oz) coconut milk

½ tsp celery salt

1 small garlic clove, crushed

1 tbsp fresh basil, finely chopped

1 tbsp fresh parsley, finely chopped

Salt and freshly ground pepper, to taste

### Mayonnaise

1 egg, room temperature

2 tbsps lemon juice

½ tsp Dijon mustard

1 cup (250ml, 8fl oz) light olive oil

½ tsp salt

## METHOD

1. To make the mayonnaise, use a stick blender to blend the egg, lemon juice and mustard together for about 10 seconds.

2. Slowly pour in the oil, blending all the while until you have a thick, creamy mayonnaise. Season with the salt to taste.

3. To make the dressing, whisk together ½ cup of the mayonnaise, coconut milk, celery salt, garlic, basil and parsley in a medium container.

4. Season to taste.

**Note:** Both mayonnaise and dressing will keep for one week in the refrigerator in an airtight container.

SERVES 2 ★ PREP 35MIN ★ COOK TIME 12MIN

# VEGGIE PESTO PIZZA ON CAULIFLOWER CRUST

## INGREDIENTS

**Crust**

1 medium head cauliflower

¼ cup (25g, 1oz) Parmesan, grated

¼ cup (30g, 1oz) mozzarella, grated

Pinch of salt

1½ tsps mixed herbs

1 egg

**Topping**

¼ cup (60g, 2oz) kale pesto sauce (see recipe page 178)

100g (3½ oz) sliced mozzarella

6 cherry tomatoes, halved

6 zucchini flowers

½ small zucchini, cut into thin 5cm (2in) long strips

½ cup (15g, ½ oz) rocket

## METHOD

1. Preheat the oven to 230°C (445°F, Gas Mark 8) and place a large flat baking tray in the oven to heat up. (Use a pizza stone if you have one.)

2. Break off the florets of cauliflower and place in a blender. Pulse until you have broken it down into breadcrumb-size pieces. You need at least 3 cups of cauliflower crumbs.

3. Place cauliflower into a microwave-proof bowl and heat on high in the microwave for 4 minutes. Dry out on a tea towel, then use the tea towel to wring as much liquid as you can out of the cauliflower crumbs.

4. Mix together thoroughly the crumbs, Parmesan, mozzarella, salt, 1 teaspoon herbs and egg.

5. Spray some baking paper with olive oil. Pat the mixture down onto some baking paper to form a 30cm (12in) pizza base. Slide the baking paper onto the baking tray and bake in the oven for 9 minutes, until it starts to lightly brown on the top.

6. Remove from the oven.

7. Spread the pesto over the base.

8. Top with slices of mozzarella.

9. Arrange the cherry tomato halves, cut side up, on top of the cheese.

10. Scatter the zucchini flowers and zucchini slices over the pizza.

11. Bake in the oven for 12 minutes or until the pizza is starting to brown at the edges.

12. Remove from the oven, scatter the rocket over the top and serve.

# PALEO RICE

## INGREDIENTS

1 medium head cauliflower, broken into florets

3 tbsps coconut oil

3 garlic cloves, crushed

1 medium carrot, diced

1 cup (170g, 6oz) fresh corn kernels

1 cup (170g, 6oz) peas

1 tsp fish sauce

1 tsp tamari sauce

Salt and pepper

Sprigs of basil, to garnish

## METHOD

1. Pulse the cauliflower in a food processor until it resembles rice.

2. Melt 1 tablespoon of the coconut oil in a large frying pan over medium heat. Add the garlic and fry for 1 minute.

3. Add the rest of the coconut oil and stir in the carrot, corn and peas, fish sauce and tamari. Cook for 5 minutes, then add the cauliflower. Stir until the cauliflower is heated through.

4. Season to taste with salt and pepper and serve garnished with basil leaves.

# CELERIAC MASH

### INGREDIENTS

700g (1½ lb) celeriac, peeled and cut into 3cm (1in) cubes

2 garlic cloves, peeled

4 cups (1L, 2pt) vegetable stock

4 tbsps butter

2 tsps Dijon mustard

Salt and pepper

8 sage leaves

### METHOD

1. Place the celeriac and garlic cloves in the stock in a large pot.

2. Boil for 10 minutes or until the celeriac is softened.

3. Drain, reserving ¼ cup of the water, and use a stick blender to puree together the celeriac and garlic into a smooth mash. Add water as needed to keep it moist.

4. Stir through half the butter and the mustard. Season to taste.

5. Heat the rest of the butter in a small saucepan over medium heat. As the butter starts to foam, add the sage leaves. Fry them for 2 minutes, then remove the leaves and butter from the saucepan.

6. Serve the mash hot with sage to garnish and butter drizzled over as well as a couple of grinds of pepper over the top.

# PICKLED VEGETABLES

## INGREDIENTS

2 cups (500ml, 1pt) water

3 tbsps pickling salt

2 sprigs fresh dill

3 garlic cloves, thinly sliced

½ cup (15g, ½ oz) watercress

4 small asparagus, cut into 3cm (1in) lengths

2 small Lebanese cucumbers, ends trimmed sliced into 5cm (2in) thin lengths

100g (3½ oz) green beans, ends trimmed cut into 3cm (1in) lengths

1 spring onion, cut into 1cm (½ in) sections

½ cup (15g, ½ oz) celery leaves, roughly chopped

1 tbsp peppercorns

1 tsp mustard seeds

## METHOD

1. Stir the water and salt together in a large bowl until salt dissolves and water is clear.

2. Put one sprig of dill, 1 tablespoon garlic slices and half the watercress in the bottom of a clean, sterilised 1L (2pt) screw-top jar.

3. Layer the asparagus, another tablespoon garlic, cucumber, beans, spring onion, celery leaves, peppercorns and mustard seeds in the jar, packing them in tightly. Top with the dill, the rest of the garlic and the rest of the watercress.

4. Gently pour the salt water into the jar, just covering the watercress, leaving 2cm (1in) of space at the top.

5. Put the lid on the jar tightly and leave it on the bench for 3-4 days. Open the jar once daily for a couple of seconds to let any gases that are forming in the fermentation process escape.

6. The vegetables will start to pickle the longer you let them ferment. Ferment them to taste, and once they're to your liking, move the jar to the refrigerator to stop the fermentation process.

**Note:** Will keep for about 2 months in the refrigerator.

# SWEET POTATO FRIES

## INGREDIENTS

1kg (2lb) sweet potatoes, peeled and cut into fries

¼ cup (60ml, 2fl oz) coconut oil

1½ tbsps thyme, chopped

3 tbsps salt

1 tbsp pepper

1 serve paprika aioli (recipe page 122)

## METHOD

1. Preheat the oven to 220°C (425°C, Gas Mark 7) and line a baking tray with baking paper.

2. Toss the fries in a large bowl with the oil, thyme, salt and pepper.

3. Place the fries on the baking tray in one layer.

4. Bake in the oven for 20 minutes or until beginning to brown on the outside.

5. Remove from the oven and serve with the aioli on the side.

# GARLIC ROASTED BEETS

## INGREDIENTS

4 medium beetroots, halved

3 large garlic cloves, peeled and halved

1 tbsp coconut oil

1 tsp balsamic vinegar

1 tsp salt

1 tsp pepper

## METHOD

1. Preheat the oven to 180°C (350°F, Gas Mark 4) and line a baking tray with baking paper.

2. Toss together the beetroot and garlic with the rest of the ingredients in a bowl.

3. Place the beetroot on the baking tray and bake for half an hour.

4. Remove from the oven and add the garlic halves.

5. Bake for another 1 hour or so until the beetroot is tender.

6. Remove from the oven and serve warm.

# DESSERTS

# LEMON POSSET

## INGREDIENTS

**Orange jelly**

5g (¼ oz) gelatin powder

¼ cup (60ml, 2fl oz) hot water

½ cup (125ml, 4fl oz) orange juice, strained

**Lemon cream**

2 cups (250g, 8oz) raw, unsalted cashews

4 cups (1L, 2pt)

3 tbsps agave syrup

2 tbsps finely ground white chia seeds

⅓ cup (80ml, 3fl oz) lemon juice

Pinch of salt

**Lemon syrup**

⅓ cup (80ml, 3fl oz) lemon juice, strained

2 tbsps agave syrup

4 thin strips lemon zest

## METHOD

1. To make the orange jelly, dissolve the gelatin in very hot, but not boiling, water. Stir until the gelatin is completely dissolved. Mix the juice into the gelatin and then let cool for 20 minutes. Pour into the bottom of two serving glasses. Place in the refrigerator for at least 6 hours to set before adding the lemon cream on top.

2. To make the lemon cream, soak the cashews in 3 cups of the water overnight.

3. Drain and place in a blender with 1 cup water, syrup, ground chia seeds, lemon juice and salt.

4. Puree for 4 minutes until completely smooth. Spoon over the set orange jelly and place in the fridge for at least 4 hours to set.

5. To make the lemon syrup, heat the lemon juice and agave syrup in a small saucepan until simmering. Let simmer on low heat for 10 minutes until the liquid is slightly reduced.

6. Chill for at least 1 hour then pour over the top of each serving glass and place a couple of strips of zest in the syrup.

# NECTARINE PIE

## INGREDIENTS

3 tbsps butter, melted

½ cup (125ml, 4fl oz) coconut milk

¼ tsp arrowroot flour

1 cup (120g, 4oz) almond meal

½ cup (50g, 2oz) coconut flour

4 eggs

¼ tsp salt

1 tsp cinnamon

¼ cup (80g, 3oz) agave syrup

5 medium white nectarines, sliced

2 tbsps brown sugar

## METHOD

1.  Preheat the oven to 180°C (350°F, Gas Mark 4) and grease a 23 x 33cm (9 x 13in) baking dish with 1 tablespoon of the melted butter.

2.  In a large mixing bowl, whisk together the melted butter, milk and arrowroot flour.

3.  Add the almond meal and coconut flour and mix through.

4.  Stir in the eggs, salt, cinnamon and agave syrup until the mixture is smooth.

5.  Pour the batter into the baking dish

6.  Place the slices of nectarine in the batter. Sprinkle the brown sugar over the top

7.  Bake for 60 minutes or it is set and the top is golden.

SERVES 4 ★ PREP 20MIN (PLUS CHILLING)

# CHOCOLATE COCONUT POTS

## INGREDIENTS

2 tbsps ground white chia seeds

¼ cup (60ml, 2fl oz) coconut milk

2 x 270ml (9fl oz) cans coconut cream

¼ cup (80g, 3oz) agave syrup

150g (5oz) dark chocolate, grated

8 fresh raspberries

Mint leaves, to garnish

## METHOD

1. Whisk together the chia seeds, coconut milk, coconut cream and agave syrup.

2. Gently heat over low heat in a medium saucepan.

3. Gently stir in the chocolate until it has just melted and combined. Do not boil the mixture.

4. Remove from heat and sweeten to taste with more agave if needed.

5. Pour into serving bowls and place them in the refrigerator overnight to chill and thicken.

6. Serve garnished with raspberries and mint leaves.

# LOW-CARB RASPBERRY CHOCOLATE CAKE

## INGREDIENTS

1½ cups (335g, 12oz) grated zucchini

2 tbsps butter, melted

2 tbsps coconut oil

½ cup (180g, 6oz) agave syrup

3 eggs

2 tsps vanilla extract

⅓ cup (30g, 1oz) coconut flour

½ cup (30g, 1oz) almond flour

1 tsp bicarbonate of soda

¼ tsp salt

2 tbsps cacao powder

100g (3½ oz) dark chocolate

1 cup (125g, 4oz) fresh raspberries

1 tbsp icing sugar

1 tbsp cornflour

## METHOD

1. Preheat the oven to 190°C (375°F, gas mark 5) and oil a 23cm (9in) round cake tin with some coconut oil.

2. Squeeze the grated zucchini to remove the liquid. Place the zucchini, butter, coconut oil, syrup, eggs and vanilla extract in a blender and blend until smooth.

3. In a large mixing bowl, stir together the coconut flour, almond flour, bicarb, salt, and cacao powder. Add the zucchini mixture and stir to combine thoroughly.

4. Break up the chocolate into pieces in a heatproof bowl. Place the bowl over a small pot of barely simmering water. Allow the chocolate to melt, stirring as little as possible.

5. Gently fold the melted chocolate into the cake mixture until mixed through.

6. Pour into the cake tin.

7. Bake for 40 minutes until the edges start to come away from the side of the tin and a skewer inserted into the middle of the cake comes out clean.

8. Remove from the tin and let cool on a wire rack.

9. Arrange the fresh raspberries over the top.

10. Mix together the sugar and cornflour then dust over the top of the cake.

# VEGAN CHOC CHIA PUDDING

### INGREDIENTS

¼ cup (30g, 1oz) cacao powder

1 ripe banana, mashed

½ tsp cinnamon

½ cup (85g, 3oz) chia seeds

1⅓ cups (330ml, 11fl oz) almond milk

1 tbsp agave syrup

¼ cup (25g, 1oz) fresh blueberries, to garnish

2 tbsps flaked almonds, to garnish

Mint leaves and chia seeds, to garnish

### METHOD

1. Mix all ingredients except garnish together in a small bowl until thoroughly combined.

2. Divide mixture between serving glasses.

3. Place in refrigerator overnight to chill and thicken.

4. Garnish with blueberries, chia seeds and mint leaves.

# COCONUT CUPCAKES

## INGREDIENTS

1½ cups (120g , 4oz) desiccated coconut

½ cup (60g, 2oz) tightly packed almond meal

2 tsps tapioca flour

¾ tsp baking powder

¼ tsp salt

3 large eggs, room temperature

⅓ cup (105g, 4oz) agave syrup

⅓ cup (80ml, 3fl oz) coconut milk

3 tbsps coconut oil

1½ cups (235g, 8oz) sugar-free dark chocolate chips

## METHOD

1. Preheat the oven to 180°C (350°F, Gas Mark 4) and line a 12-hole cupcake tin with cupcake liners.

2. In a large bowl, stir together the desiccated coconut, almond meal, tapioca flour, baking powder and salt and set aside.

3. In another bowl, mix together the eggs, agave syrup, coconut milk and coconut oil until just combined.

4. Add to the dry ingredients and mix together thoroughly.

5. Fill the cupcake liners so that they're about half-full. Top with the chocolate chips

6. Bake in the oven for 20 minutes or until a toothpick inserted in the middle of a cupcake comes out clean.

7. Let them cool for 2 minutes, then remove the cupcakes from the tin and place on a wire rack to cool completely.

MAKES 12 ★ PREP 25MIN ★ COOK TIME 55MIN

# PUMPKIN MAGIC BARS

## INGREDIENTS

2 cups (270g, 9oz) butternut pumpkin pieces, peeled and cut into 2cm (1in) cubes

1 large ripe banana

½ cup (85g, 3oz) dates, chopped

¼ cup (40g, 1½ oz) dark chocolate, chopped

⅓ cup (80ml, 3fl oz) coconut oil, melted

¼ cup (80g, 3oz) agave syrup

1 cup (30g, 1oz) almond meal

¼ cup (25g, 1oz) coconut flour

1 tbsp cinnamon

½ tbsp allspice

1 tbsp vanilla extract

½ tsp bicarbonate of soda

1½ cups (130g, 4½ oz) shredded coconut

2 tsps light brown sugar

## METHOD

1. Preheat the oven to 180°C (350°F, Gas Mark 4) and grease a 28 x 23cm (11 x 9in)  baking dish with coconut oil.

2. Boil the pumpkin cubes in water in a small pot for 15 minutes or until the pumpkin is soft. Drain, then mash until you get a rough puree.

3. In a large mixing bowl, mash the banana and dates together until roughly combined.

4. Stir through the pumpkin mash, chocolate, oil and agave syrup.

5. Add the almond meal, coconut flour, cinnamon, allspice, vanilla and bicarb. Mix together well until all ingredients are combined

6. Spread out evenly in the baking dish.

7. Top with the shredded coconut and sprinkle the brown sugar over the top.

8. Bake for 40 minutes, until the top is lightly browned.

9. Cool, then cut into bars.

**Note:** Will keep in the refrigerator in a sealed container for a week.

SERVES 8 ★ PREP 30min ★ COOK TIME 50min

# PLUM AND ALMOND COBBLER

## INGREDIENTS

4 tbsps butter

4 tbsps coconut oil

½ cup (180g, 6oz) agave syrup

3 tbsps maple syrup

⅓ cup (100ml, 3½ fl oz) coconut cream

1 tsp vanilla extract

¾ cup (60g, 2oz) desiccated coconut

3 eggs, room temperature

1½ cups (180g, 6oz) almond meal

½ cup (50g, 2oz) coconut flour

800g (1¾ lb) blood plums, stones removed, cut into sections

## METHOD

1.  Preheat the oven to 180°C (350°F, Gas Mark 4) and grease and line a 23cm (9in) springform cake tin with baking paper.

2.  Using electric beaters, beat together the butter, coconut oil, half the agave syrup, maple syrup, coconut cream, vanilla and dessicated coconut until pale and creamy.

3.  Add the eggs, one at a time. Beat until mixed. Gently fold in the almond meal and coconut flour.

4.  Pour the batter into the tin. Arrange the plums, skin down, on top of the batter. Drizzle the remaining agave syrup over the top of the nectarines.

5.  Bake for 50 minutes or until a skewer inserted into the centre comes out clean.

6.  Remove from tin and place on a wire rack to cool slightly. Serve warm.

# PALEO APPLE CRUMBLE

### INGREDIENTS

5 apples, use red ones such as pink lady or sundowner

½ tsp lemon juice

1½ cups (180g, 6oz) almond meal

¼ cup (30g, 1oz) pecans, roughly chopped

¼ cup (30g, 1oz) walnuts, roughly chopped

½ cup (40g, 1½ oz) shredded coconut

1 tbsp cinnamon

1 tbsp allspice

½ tsp ground cardamom

¼ tsp salt

⅓ cup (70ml, 2½ fl oz) agave syrup

5 tbsps coconut oil, melted

1 tbsp grated lemon rind

2 tbsps light brown sugar

### METHOD

1. Preheat the oven to 150°C (300°F, Gas Mark 2) and lightly oil a 30cm (12in) round pie dish with coconut oil.

2. Peel and core the apples and cut into small 1cm (½ in) chunks and place in a medium-sized bowl.

3. Gently stir the lemon juice into the apples then place the apples into the bottom of the baking dish.

4. Add the almond meal, pecans, walnuts, coconut, cinnamon, allspice, cardamom and salt in a medium bowl and mix thoroughly.

5. Stir together the agave syrup and coconut oil in a small bowl. Add to the dry ingredients and mix together thoroughly.

6. Spread the mixture evenly over the top of the apples. Sprinkle with the lemon rind and brown sugar.

7. Bake in the oven for about 50 minutes, or until the crumble has turned golden brown. Serve warm.

# COCONUT CHIA POTS WITH LOW-CARB CARAMEL SAUCE

## INGREDIENTS

1 cup (120g, 4oz) walnuts, roughly chopped

½ cup (85g, 3oz) chia seeds

1 cup (250ml, 8fl oz) coconut milk

2 cups (500ml, 1pt) coconut water

2 tbsps agave syrup

3 tbsps maple syrup

1 tsp vanilla extract

½ tsp salt

1 ripe banana, sliced

## METHOD

1. Dry fry the walnuts in a small frying pan over medium heat for 2 minutes until just starting to brown. Remove immediately from the pan and set aside.

2. Mix together the chia seeds, coconut milk, 1 cup of the coconut water and agave syrup in a bowl. Cover and place in the refrigerator for at least 4 hours, preferably overnight.

3. To make the caramel sauce, place the rest of the coconut water, the maple syrup, vanilla extract and salt in a medium saucepan over medium-high heat.

4. Keep stirring until the mixture boils. Reduce the heat to low and add the banana slices.

5. Keep stirring for 10 minutes or until the sauce thickens and darkens.

6. Remove from the heat and allow to cool for 10 minutes before using.

7. Distribute half the chia pudding mix between two serving glasses. Layer each with a quarter of the banana caramel sauce and half a tablespoon of walnuts.

8. Repeat with the pudding, banana caramel sauce and walnuts.

9. Serve garnished with extra walnuts.

**SERVES 4 ★ PREP 15 MIN (PLUS REFRIGERATION)**

# BERRY SORBET

## INGREDIENTS

4 cups (500g, 1lb 2oz)
mixed fresh berries

½ cup (180g, 6oz) honey

1 cup (250ml, 8fl oz)
coconut cream

Pinch of salt

2 tbsps coconut oil

## METHOD

1.  Add the berries to a food processor and pulse a few times.

2.  Add the honey, coconut cream, salt and oil.

3.  Blend until smooth.

4.  Pour into a large bowl, cover with plastic wrap and place in the freezer for 1 hour.

5.  Remove from the freezer and blend again until smooth.

6.  Place into an airtight container and freeze for at least 4 hours, preferably overnight.

7.  Serve chilled.

# BERRY POPSICLES

## INGREDIENTS

2 cups (200g, 6oz) blueberries (fresh or frozen)

1 tbsp fresh mint, finely chopped

1 cup (250ml, 8fl oz) Greek yoghurt

½ cup (125ml, 4fl oz) water

2 tbsps honey

6 wooden icy-pole sticks

1 x 6-hole icy-pole mould

## METHOD

1. Place the berries in a blender with the mint and blend until smooth.

2. Mix yoghurt, water and honey in a large bowl and stir through the berry mixture.

3. Fill the icy-pole moulds to 3mm (⅛ in) from the top.

4. Place a wooden stick in the middle with half sticking out.

5. Transfer to the freezer and freeze for 8 hours.

6. Remove from moulds and eat cold.

# RAW BLUEBERRY CHEESECAKE

## INGREDIENTS

### Crust

1 cup (120g, 4oz) almond meal

1 cup (120g, 4oz) ground hazelnuts

2 tbsps agave syrup

70g (2½ oz) butter, melted

1 tsp allspice

### Filling

3 cups (375g, 12oz) cashews

¾ cup (185ml, 6fl oz) lemon juice

¾ cup (260g, 9oz) honey

¾ cup (185ml, 6fl oz) coconut cream

2 cups (200g, 7oz) blueberries, frozen

1 tbsp vanilla extract

Water, as required

### Sauce

80g (3oz) unsweetened dark chocolate, melted

1 tsp cacao powder

1 cup (125g, 4oz) coconut cream

2 tbsps agave syrup

½ tsp vanilla extract

Pinch of salt

½ cup (60g, 2oz) roasted peanuts, to garnish

1 cup (200g, 7oz) fresh blueberries, to garnish

## METHOD

1. Place the crust ingredients into a bowl and stir thoroughly to combine.

2. Press into a 23cm (9in) round cake tin. Transfer to the refrigerator to chill.

3. To make the filling, place the ingredients into a blender and pulse to loosen up the ingredients. Then blend for 1 minute or until you have a smooth puree, adding water only if needed to loosen the mixture for blending.

4. Pour the berry mixture into the cake tin over the crust.

5. Place the cake in the freezer for at least 4 hours, preferably overnight.

6. To make the chocolate sauce, melt the chocolate in a small, heavy-based saucepan or double boiler over low heat. Add the remaining sauce ingredients and gently stir together until combined.

7. Let the cheesecake defrost for 30 minutes before serving.

8. Before serving, arrange the peanuts and blueberries over the cheesecake and drizzle the chocolate sauce over the top.

# PALEO CRUNCH BARS

## INGREDIENTS

120g (4 oz) dark unsweetened chocolate, roughly chopped

1½ tbsps coconut oil

½ tsp vanilla extract

½ cup (60g, 2oz) walnuts, roughly chopped

½ cup (60g, 2oz) pecans, roughly chopped

½ cup (40g, 1½ oz) shredded coconut

2 tsps cacao powder

½ cup (85g, 3oz) chia seeds

¼ tsp salt

1 cup (175g, 6oz) Medjool dates, pitted and chopped

## METHOD

1. In a small, heavy-based saucepan or double boiler melt the chocolate, coconut oil and vanilla extract over low heat. Remove from heat and set aside.

2. Pour the chopped nuts into a small mixing bowl and add the shredded coconut, cacao powder, chia seeds and salt. Stir to combine.

3. Place the dates in a food processor and blend to a paste. Add the melted chocolate and gently blend to mix through. Add the rest of the ingredients and pulse slightly to just combine.

4. Line a slice tin with baking paper and press the mixture into the tin.

5. Place in the refrigerator to cool and harden for at least 2 hours.

6. Cut into bars.

**Note:** Will keep for up to a week in an airtight container in the refrigerator.

# CHOCOLATE ENERGY BALLS

## INGREDIENTS

¾ cup (90g, 4oz) unsweetened dark chocolate, roughly chopped

1 cup (115g, 4oz) almonds

¾ cup (90g, 3oz) pistachios

2 tbsps ground flaxseed

2 tbsps chia seeds

1 tbsp maple syrup

1 cup (160g, 6oz) Medjool dates, pitted

1 tbsp coconut oil

1 tbsp cacao powder

½ cup (40g, 1½ oz) coconut flakes

## METHOD

1. Place the chocolate, almonds, half the pistachios, flaxseed and chia seeds in a food processor. Blitz for 1 minute, until a breadcrumb consistency forms.

2. Add the maple syrup, dates, coconut oil and cacao powder and blend for a further 1 minute until a dough forms.

3. Using hands, form the mixture into little balls.

4. Use a spice blender to pulse the remaining pistachios until they're almost a fine powder. Place in a small, shallow dish.

5. Roll half the balls in the coconut and the rest in the pistachio powder.

6. Place in the refrigerator for 1 hour to chill.

# WHITE CHOCOLATE TART

## INGREDIENTS

### Crust

2 cups (240g, 8oz) almond meal

2 tbsps maple syrup

5 tbsps (70g, 2½ oz) butter, melted

½ tsp ground cardamom

### Filling

2 tbsps chia seeds

520g (1lb 2oz) soft tofu

½ cup (125ml, 4fl oz) coconut oil

1 tsp vanilla extract

½ tsp salt

½ cup (125ml, 4fl oz) coconut cream

½ cup (80g, 3oz) palm sugar, grated

¾ cup (60g, 2oz) desiccated coconut

200g (7oz) white cooking chocolate

### Garnish

1 mango, cut into small cubes

½ cup (60g, 2oz) raspberries

Edible flowers (e.g. borage, violets)

3 tbsps puffed rice

## METHOD

1. Place the crust ingredients into a bowl and stir thoroughly to combine.

2. Press into a 30cm (12in) round flan tin. Place in the refrigerator to chill.

3. Use a spice grinder to blitz the chia seeds into fine powder.

4. In a food processor, blend together the tofu, oil, vanilla, salt, chia powder, coconut cream and palm sugar.

5. Pour into a bowl and stir through the coconut until thoroughly combined.

6. Melt the chocolate in a small, heavy-based saucepan or double boiler over low heat.

7. Gently stir the chocolate into the filling mixture.

8. Pour the filling into the tin over the base, but reserve about 2 tablespoons of the filling.

9. Chill in the refrigerator for at least 4 hours, preferably overnight.

10. Before serving, pipe some of the reserved filling on top of the cake as decoration. Arrange the mango, raspberries and flowers on top the cake and sprinkle over the puffed rice.

# MATCHA SQUARES

## INGREDIENTS

250g (9oz) unsalted butter, melted

2 eggs

¼ cup (30g, 1oz) matcha green tea powder, plus 3 tbsps for dusting

1 cup (125g, 4oz) flour

¾ cup (90g, 3oz) almond meal

½ cup (180g, 6oz) agave syrup

½ cup (235g, 8oz) white chocolate chips

¼ tsp vanilla extract

## METHOD

1. Preheat oven to 180°C (350°F, Gas Mark 4). Grease and line a slice tin with baking paper

2. Pour melted butter into the bowl of a stand mixer. Allow to cool for 4 minutes then add eggs and matcha powder to the bowl and beat on low until combined.

3. Add flour, almond meal, agave, chocolate chips and vanilla extract and mix until just incorporated.

4. Pour batter into prepared pan and spread evenly with a spatula.

5. Place in the oven and bake for 20 minutes until firm to the touch.

6. Remove from the oven and place tin on a wire rack to cool.

7. Sift the extra matcha over the top before cutting into squares.

# SPICED PEARS

## INGREDIENTS

4 firm, medium-sized
buerre bosc pears

¼ cup (60ml, 2fl oz)
apple juice

¼ cup (60ml, 2fl oz)
water

2 tbsps honey

1 tbsp butter

1 tbsp coconut oil

1 stick cinnamon

2 star anise

4 curls lemon peel

## METHOD

1.  Preheat the oven to 200°C (400°F, Gas Mark 6).

2.  Peel the pears, keeping the stem intact, and place in a medium-
    sized, deep-sided baking dish.

3.  Place the juice, water, honey, butter, coconut oil, cinnamon stick
    and star anise in a small saucepan and heat until simmering.

4.  Pour the sauce over the pears.

5.  Bake in the oven for 35 minutes. Remove the cinnamon and star
    anise.

6.  Allow pears to sit for 5 minutes, then place each pear in a serving
    bowl, drizzle with the extra sauce and serve garnished with a lemon
    peel curl.

# LEMON BARS

## INGREDIENTS

1 cup (120g, 4oz) almond meal

⅓ cup (30g, 1oz) plus 2 tbsps coconut flour

¼ tsp salt

2 tbsps grapeseed oil

2 tbsps agave syrup

½ tsp vanilla extract

**Lemon curd filling**

½ cup (125ml, 4fl oz) lemon juice

1 lemon, zested

½ cup (180g, 6oz) agave syrup

5 eggs, plus 1 egg yolk

1 tsp coconut flour, sifted

1 tbsp tapioca flour, for dusting

1 lemon, zested into small curls

## METHOD

1. Preheat the oven to 180°C (350°F, Gas Mark 4) and line a slice tin with baking paper.

2. Add the almond meal, coconut flour and salt into a food processor. Pulse a few times to mix together.

3. Add the oil and give another couple of pulses to mix through.

4. Then add the agave and vanilla and pulse until combined. Press the mixture into the base of the slice tin.

5. Prick the base with a fork, then place in the oven and bake for 8 minutes. Use baking beads if you have them. Remove from the oven and set aside.

6. To make the filling, whisk together the lemon juice, the zest, agave syrup, eggs and egg yolk until combined. Whisk the coconut flour through thoroughly.

7. Pour the filling into the tin over the crust and place back in the oven for 20 minutes or until the centre is mostly set, but still slightly wobbly.

8. Cool for 30 minutes, then place in the refrigerator to set for at least 4 hours, preferably overnight. Cut into desired bar sizes.

9. Dust with the tapioca flour and garnish with curls of lemon zest.

# LEMON CURD MACAROONS

## INGREDIENTS

1½ cups (375g, 13oz) lemon curd filling (see recipe page 214)

**Macaroons**

3 cups (270g, 9oz) shredded coconut

⅔ cup (160ml, 5fl oz) coconut milk

1 egg white

½ tsp vanilla extract

1 tsp fresh lemon juice

1 tsp lemon zest

⅛ tsp salt

## METHOD

1. Preheat the oven to 160°C (325°F, Gas Mark 3) and line a large baking tray with baking paper.

2. Add all the macaroon ingredients to a large mixing bowl and stir to combine thoroughly.

3. For each macaroon, scoop out a golf-ball sized portion of mixture, place on the tray and make a small depression in the centre. Make the depressions large enough to hold about a tablespoon of curd later on.

4. Bake the macaroons in the oven for 20 minutes or until browned.

5. Let them cool for 10 minutes, then fill each with a tablespoon of curd.

# ORANGE ALMOND CAKE

## INGREDIENTS

2 medium oranges

4 eggs

½ cup (180g, 6oz) agave syrup

1 tbsp maple syrup

2 tsps baking powder

1 tsp vanilla extract

3 cups (330g, 12oz) almond meal

1 tsp ground cardamom

¼ cup (30g, 1oz) flaked almonds, to garnish

## METHOD

1. Preheat the oven to 180°C (350°F, Gas Mark 4) and grease a 22cm (8½ in) round cake tin.

2. Place the oranges (unpeeled) in a medium saucepan and cover with water. Bring to a boil, then simmer for 1 hour. Remove from the saucepan and let cool for 15 minutes.

3. Roughly chop up the oranges into large segments and remove any pips.

4. Place the oranges, eggs, agave syrup, maple syrup, baking powder and vanilla into a blender and mix until smooth.

5. Pour the orange mix into a large mixing bowl and stir through the almond meal and cardamom.

6. Pour the cake batter into the tin.

7. Bake in the oven for 1½ hours or until the cake is cooked and a skewer inserted into the middle comes out clean.

8. Garnish with the flaked almonds.

# DECADENT CARROT CAKE

## INGREDIENTS

1½ cups (150g, 5oz) almond flour

¾ cup (165g, 6oz) stevia powder

2 tsps baking powder

1 tsp cinnamon

1 tsp ground ginger

¼ tsp salt

¾ cup (185ml, 6fl oz) soy milk

2 tsps vanilla extract

¼ cup (60ml, 2fl oz) coconut oil

2 eggs

1 cup (50g, 2oz) carrot, grated

1 cup (125g, 4oz) whole pecans, plus 2 tsps chopped

½ cup (40g, 1½ oz) coconut flakes

**Icing**

½ cup (130g, 4oz) soft tofu

2 tbsps chia seeds, ground

½ cup (125ml, 4fl oz) coconut cream

½ cup (60g, 2oz) cashews, chopped

2 tbsps stevia powder

1 tsp salt

## METHOD

1. To make the icing, place all the icing ingredients in a blender and puree until smooth and thick. Place in the refrigerator to chill for at least 1 hour

2. Preheat the oven to 180°C (350°F, Gas Mark 4) and oil a 20cm (8in) round cake tin with coconut oil.

3. In a large bowl, stir together the flour, stevia, baking powder, spices and salt. Then add the milk, vanilla, oil, eggs and carrot and stir through until thoroughly combined.

4. Bake in the oven for 40 minutes or until a skewer inserted in the middle comes out clean.

5. Turn out onto a wire rack and let cool for at least 30 minutes.

6. Then carefully slice the cake in half so you have two rounds.

7. Spread ¼ cup of the icing under the bottom of one cake half. Place that half on your serving plate. Use a third of the icing to cover the top of the same cake half. Place the other cake half on top and ice the top of the cake with the rest of the icing.

8. Decorate with pecans, chopped pecans and coconut flakes. Place in the refrigerator for at least 2 hours to chill.

# CHIA CINNAMON PUDDING POTS

### INGREDIENTS

4 tbsps chia seeds

1 cup (250ml, 8fl oz) almond milk

2 tbsps agave syrup

½ tsp cinnamon

½ cup (125ml, 4fl oz) Greek yoghurt

¾ cup (75g, 3oz) fresh blueberries

### METHOD

1. Mix together the chia seeds, almond milk, agave syrup and cinnamon in a bowl.

2. Cover and place in the refrigerator overnight.

3. Divide the chia pudding mix between two serving glasses.

4. Dollop half the yoghurt over each.

5. Top with fresh blueberries.

# BANANA CINNAMON ICE CREAM

## INGREDIENTS

½ cup (125ml, 4fl oz) coconut cream

2 tbsps coconut oil, melted and cooled

1 tsp vanilla extract

½ tsp cinnamon

4 large ripe bananas (sliced and frozen)

Pinch of salt

Walnuts, to garnish

## METHOD

1. In a small bowl, stir together the coconut cream, coconut oil, vanilla extract and cinnamon.

2. Place the banana and salt in a food processor and begin to blend. When small crumbs form, slowly pour in the liquid coconut mixture through the top of the machine, as it is still running. When the mixture is creamy, it is ready.

3. For soft serve ice cream, eat immediately. For a firmer scoop texture, place in the freezer for 3-4 hours.

   **Note:** Don't overblend or the mixture will start to go gooey, losing its genuine ice-cream texture.

# INDEX

First Published in 2018 by Herron Book Distributors Pty Ltd
14 Manton St
Morningside
QLD 4170
www.herronbooks.com

Custom book production by Captain Honey Pty Ltd
12 Station St
Bangalow
NSW 2479
www.captainhoney.com.au

Cataloguing-in-Publication. A catalogue record for this book is available from the National Library of Australia

ISBN 978-0-947163-96-9

Images used under license from Shutterstock.com except
Printed and bound in China by 1010 Printing International Limited

5  4  3      19  20  21  22

## NOTES FOR THE READER

Preparation, cooking times and serving sizes vary according to the skill, agility and appetite of the cook and should be used as a guide only.

All reasonable efforts have been made to ensure the accuracy of the content in this book. Information in this book is not intended as a substitute for medical advice. The author and publisher cannot and do not accept any legal duty of care or responsibility in relation to the content in this book, and disclaim any liabilities relating to its use.